edexcel
advancing learning, changing lives

ResultsPlusRevision

Edexcel GCSE
History B
Schools History Project
Unit 1A, 2B, 2C & 3A

With diagnostic tests on CD-ROM

A PEARSON COMPANY

How to use the book and CD-ROM

Welcome to the ResultsPlus Revision guide for Edexcel's Schools History Project.

This book will help you prepare for your exams with more confidence. It contains the key information you need to know, along with plenty of practice questions and tips from the people that write and mark your exams.

But before you start revising, why not take a diagnostic test? This will help you to identify what you already know and where you need to improve.

Insert the CD-ROM and follow the easy installation instructions. Then choose a test from the Tests menu. You can take each diagnostic test as many times as you want! Your latest results will be saved on your computer.

After taking a test, click on the Results tab. The Analysis screen shows your scores, question-by-question. Test review lets you look back at your answers and compare them with the correct answers. And your personalised skills map shows you how you performed in each area of your course. By copying across the red, amber and green symbols to the revision tracker at the front of your book, you can see where to spend more time revising...

The book is divided into the units and topics from your specification.

Each section explains what you need to know about that topic. We've also included some helpful ResultsPlus features.

There are 6 tests on the CD. You only need to take 4 of them.

Test 1 covers Unit 1. Tests 2–3 cover the Extension options. Before you take these tests you need to pick the extension study that you have been taught, one of:

- Medicine and public health from Roman Britain to c1350
- Public health c1350 to the present day.

Tests 4 and 5 cover two Depth Studies:

- The American West c1840–c1845
- Life in Germany c1919–c1945.

You only need take the one you have studied.

Test 6 covers Unit 3: The transformation of surgery c1845–c1918.

SuperFacts and Answering questions

There are two types of pages in this book. SuperFacts pages tell you what you need to learn. Answering questions pages help you practice the skills you need to do well.

SuperFacts all you need to learn, broken down into 20–25 'SuperFacts'.

Section summary gives you a quick overview of the topic.

What you need to do tells you how to answer each question and get top marks.

ResultsPlus boxes give you tips based on previous exams.

How you do it shows you how to do it.

Core summary
During this period, people had different ideas about the causes of disease. Many people believed in supernatural causes; that God, witches or the position of the planets sent disease. Others, however, believed in various natural causes, including an imbalance in the body's 'humours' (an idea first outlined by the Ancient Greeks) and 'bad' air.

Doctors treated disease according to their ideas about what had caused it. Supernatural diseases were treated with prayers, magical charms or offerings to the gods. Natural diseases were treated with various herbal and other cures, including 'bleeding' patients and 'purging' them by making them vomit or causing diarrhoea.

Medicine was affected by outside influences as well as ideas about disease and treatment. For some time the Christian Church banned dissection of human corpses. This prevented doctors from finding out how the human body worked. On the other hand, technological advances made during the Renaissance helped medicine. For example, the invention of printing meant more books were made more cheaply and people could spread medical ideas more easily.

SuperFacts Core Topic 1
Medicine c1350–c1750

SuperFacts are the key bits of information. Learn them and ask someone to test you.

Life expectancy in the 1350s was about 30 years in England (the rich often lived longer); now it is about 80. On average, three of every five children died in childhood: one at birth (many mothers died then too), another within the year and the third before adulthood. Most died of disease caused by poor living conditions or malnutrition. ● p.5

Medical treatment was provided by doctors (who trained and passed exams and were expensive), apothecaries (trained in making medicines), barber-surgeons (untrained, mainly practical treatment) and local people known to be good at herbal cures. Who you went to depended on the illness and what you could pay. ● p.10–11

Hospitals at this time were mostly places where the old were cared for by monks or nuns. Some hospitals cared for people with particular diseases such as leprosy. ● p.10–11

The Four Humours was a theory of disease introduced by the Ancient Greeks. They believed that your body had four different liquids (blood, phlegm, yellow bile and black bile) that had to be kept in balance. If they went out of balance, this affected your health and your behaviour. ● p.6

Galen, a Roman doctor working in the 2nd century CE, developed a 'theory of opposites' to treat a patient whose humours were out of balance. ● p.6–7

Balancing the humours If a person had too much phlegm (linked to moisture and winter), they should eat hot, peppery food. Galen wrote many books about medicine and surgery that summed up medical ideas at the time. Galen believed in bloodletting as a treatment and a preventative measure. ● p.6–7

The first medical school was set up in Salerno in the 10th century. Galen's books were used to train doctors, who were given no practical experience and did no further research. ● p.7

Natural remedies (such as herbal cures) were also used by medieval doctors. Herbs were burned on the fire (or carried in metal balls called pomanders) to act against 'bad' air. Spices and stones (such as bezoar) were also ground up as medicine. ● p.7

Some doctors blamed the planets for disease They studied the planets' movements to decide how to treat patients. *A vade mecum* was a handbook for doctors that included astrology charts and charts of different colours of urine to use for diagnosis. ● p.7

The Black Death (also called bubonic plague) swept across Europe in the 14th century, reaching England in 1348. It was carried by fleas on black rats and got into a person's bloodstream when the flea bit them. People got a fever and had swellings in their groin and armpits that became black bruises. About a third of the population died. ● p.8

Causes suggested for the Black Death God's punishment for human sins; a bad positioning of the planets Mars, Jupiter and Saturn; 'bad' air (caused by dirt in the streets or the breath of those affected); plots by witches or Jews. Many people tried several of these. None worked. ● p.8–9

Cures suggested for the Black Death Prayer; burning or smelling herbs and spices; isolation; cleaning rubbish off the streets; flagellation (whipping as a penance for sins); wearing lucky charms. ● p.9

The Renaissance was when people rediscovered Ancient Greek and Roman ideas; testing by experiment replaced accepting information in books. The Church split into Catholic and Protestant during the Reformation and lost some authority. ● p.12

The Medical Renaissance was the change in medical ideas affected by Renaissance thinking and inventions that lasted into the 17th century. It was helped by printing, the weakening of Church authority and various technological inventions that came from scientific experimentation. ● p.12–13

Dissection of human corpses became more common as people questioned old ideas and began to investigate scientifically. Leonardo da Vinci and Vesalius made detailed drawings of the inside of the human body. Instead of using Galen's surgical instructions (based on pigs), some doctors used diagrams based on the human body. ● p.12

Vesalius published *Fabric of the Human Body* in 1543. Based on human dissections, it showed that Galen's surgical books were wrong about the structure of the human heart (he said the septum had holes that blood passed through; it doesn't), liver (he said it had five lobes; it has two) and lower jaw (he said it had two bones; it has one). ● p.12

Printing meant that many more books could be produced, faster and more cheaply, than by copying by hand. Printed medical texts (such as Vesalius' *Fabric of the Human Body*) spread medical knowledge all over Europe. This encouraged further investigations and experiments. ● p.12

Scientific experimentation became popular. Groups such as the Royal Society in London (whose patron was King Charles II) exchanged ideas with similar societies in other countries. These groups encouraged observation and accurate recording in all experiments, including those with medical applications. ● p.12

William Harvey developed his ideas about the way blood circulates around the body after learning how pumps work. In 1628, he published *An Anatomical Account of the Motion of the Heart and Blood in Animals* explaining his ideas. ● p.13

Better equipment (such as microscope lenses that gave bigger, clearer magnification) helped scientists. Bacteria were discovered by Antonie van Leeuwenhoek, who described these 'animalcules' to the Royal Society in London in 1673. ● p.13

New ideas were not always accepted Many people were reluctant to change their thinking. Harvey's book was not used in medical schools until 40 years after it was first printed; surgeons were still trained using Galen's theories. When the bubonic plague returned in 1665, many of the treatments used were the same as in 1350. ● p.13

New ideas were not always immediately useful Harvey's ideas about circulation were interesting, but did not directly improve thinking about the cause and treatment of disease. Most ordinary doctors did not even hear of Harvey's ideas, or Vesalius'. They continued to treat according to the Four Humours or astrology. ● p.13

New ideas were not always linked to disease. Van Leeuwenhoek's bacteria were seen as an example of how microscopes had improved. Nobody at the time made the link between bacteria and the causes of disease. ● p.13

---

edexcel :: key terms

dissection Cutting up something dead, carefully, to see what is inside.

Four Humours The name given to a theory, first advanced by the Ancient Greeks, that the body is made up of four different liquids ('humours') which must be kept in balance, otherwise a person becomes ill.

miasma The word often used by medieval doctors to describe 'bad' air, which was full of bad smells, from dirt and decay to sewage.

ResultsPlus Top tip

Knowing the theory of the Four Humours is vital to your study of medicine. Learn the chart on p.6 of the textbook. If you find it difficult to learn all four humours, learn two of them very thoroughly and always give them as your examples.

Need more help?
You can find a longer explanation of each SuperFact in your Edexcel textbook, *Schools History Project: Medicine and Surgery*. Look for this symbol ●, which will give you the page number.

Need more help? gives details of where to look in the main student book for more information.

Edexcel key terms words and phrases that you need to recall and use in your exams.

Now test yourself
Practise a full examination answer. Write in each of the boxes to complete the answer.
Use the SuperFacts on the right to help you.

In what ways did the Romans use hygiene to avoid illness?

One way the Romans used hygiene to avoid illness was bathing.
(iii)

Another way the Romans used hygiene to avoid illness was public toilets.
(iv)

Another way the Romans used hygiene to avoid illness was by... (v)
(vi)

SuperFacts

Romans believed in keeping clean, using clean water and avoiding swampy places and 'bad' air. This was based on their observations that dirt and unhealthy places were linked to disease, although they did not know what the link was.

Roman public baths charged a fee. Some were cheap and basic, others expensive and luxurious. All provided at least a changing room, an exercise hall, a warm room, a hot pool and a cold pool. Romans did not use soap; they oiled themselves then scraped off the oil and dirt with a strigil (a metal scraper).

Wealthy Romans had private baths attached to their homes for the family and visitors to use. However, many men still visited the public baths because they were meeting places as well as somewhere to get clean.

Roman towns had public toilets with running water which drained away into sewers or, in less important and wealthy towns, open drains. Sewage was kept separate from fresh water, even if drains were not covered.

Roman towns had fresh water piped from a clean water supply. Towns had street fountains or wells where people could collect water. Water carriers also sold it.

ResultsPlus Top tip

Make sure that the information you use is **relevant to the focus of the question.** Don't just say *The Romans had public toilets with drains to take away the sewage.* Only answers that explain **how this helped to prevent illness** will reach the top level.

The answer
You can find suggested answers to the tasks numbered (i), (ii), etc., on page 42.

Selected SuperFacts are repeated on the questions page to help you learn how to use them to support your answers – this is what many of the marks are for in the exam.

Test yourself gives you *practice* so you can be sure you know how to do it. The answers are on another page.

Unit 1 Schools History Project Development Study

Unit 1A: Medicine and treatment c1350 to present day

Core Topics

1.1 Medicine and treatment c1350–1750 p.10

- ☒ ⑦ ☑ Ideas about the cause of disease: belief in the supernatural; the search for a natural explanation of illness
- ☒ ⑦ ☑ Approaches to the treatment and prevention of disease and illness
- ☒ ⑦ ☑ The influence of the Church and the Renaissance on medicine
- ☒ ⑦ ☑ Medicine and treatment c1350–1750 (synthesis)

1.2 Medicine and treatment c1750–1900 p.12

- ☒ ⑦ ☑ Ideas about the cause of disease: the development of the germ theory; the identification of microbes
- ☒ ⑦ ☑ Approaches to the treatment and prevention of diseases and illness; the development of vaccination
- ☒ ⑦ ☑ The influence of industrialisation and science on changes in medicine
- ☒ ⑦ ☑ Medicine and treatment c1750–1900 (synthesis)

1.3 Medicine and treatment 1900 to present day p.16

- ☒ ⑦ ☑ Ideas about the cause of disease: growing understanding of microbes and of genetic conditions
- ☒ ⑦ ☑ Approaches to the treatment and prevention of diseases and illness; high-tech medicine
- ☒ ⑦ ☑ The influence of science and technology on changes in medicine
- ☒ ⑦ ☑ Medicine and treatment 1900 to present day (synthesis)

Extension Topics

1.4 Medicine and public health from Roman Britain to c1350 p.20

- ☒ ⑦ ☑ Ideas about the causes of disease
- ☒ ⑦ ☑ Approaches to the treatment and prevention of diseases and illness
- ☒ ⑦ ☑ The influence of science and technology on changes in medicine
- ☒ ⑦ ☑ Medicine and treatment from Roman Britain to c1350 (synthesis)

1.5 Public health c1350 to present day p.22

- ☒ ⑦ ☑ Problems of public health and their attempted solutions
- ☒ ⑦ ☑ The impact of industrialisation and the reasons for the growth of government intervention
- ☒ ⑦ ☑ The changing nature of state provision
- ☒ ⑦ ☑ Public health from c1350 to present day (synthesis)

Unit 3 Schools History Project Source Enquiry

Option 3A: The transformation of surgery c1845-c1918

3A.1 Dealing with pain p.48

- ☒ ⑦ ☑ Developments in anaesthetics; the work of Simpson

3A.2 Dealing with infection p.49

- ☒ ⑦ ☑ Battle against infection, developments in antiseptics; the work of Lister

3A.3 Dealing with blood loss p.50

- ☒ ⑦ ☑ Blood types, blood banks, transfusions

3A.4 Factors influencing developments in surgery p.51

- ☒ ⑦ ☑ The role of science and technology; war; communications

Unit 2 Schools History Project Depth Study

The Unit 1 Exam:
Medicine and treatment

Write your name here

Surname		Other names

Centre Number   Candidate Number

Edexcel GCSE

History B (Schools History Project)
Unit 1: Schools History Project Development Study
Option 1A: Medicine and treatment

Sample Assessment Material	Paper Reference
Time: 1 hour 15 minutes	**5HB01/1A**

You do not need any other materials.   Total Marks

Instructions

- Use **black** ink or ball-point pen.
- **Fill in the boxes** at the top of this page with your name, centre number and candidate number.
- Answer Questions 1 and 2, **EITHER** Question 3 **OR** 4 and then **EITHER** Question 5(a) and 5(b) **OR** 6(a) and 6(b).
- Answer the questions in the spaces provided
  – *there may be more space than you need.*

Information

- The total mark for this paper is 50.
- The marks for **each** question are shown in brackets
  – *use this as a guide as to how much time to spend on each question.*
- Questions labelled with an **asterisk** (*) are ones where the quality of your written communication will be assessed
  – *you should take particular care with your spelling, punctuation and grammar, as well as the clarity of expression, on these questions.*

Advice

- Read each question carefully before you start to answer it.
- Keep an eye on the time.
- Try to answer every question.
- Check your answers if you have time at the end.

Turn over ▶

N35680A
©2008 Edexcel Limited.
2/2/2

N 3 5 6 8 0 A 0 1 0 8

edexcel
advancing learning, changing lives

Edexcel GCSE in History B   Sample Assessment Materials   © Edexcel Limited 2008   5

Unit 1 is a Development Study – in it you study one theme in British history over 700–2,000 years, depending on the Extension Study you take. In this book, the theme is *Medicine and treatment*.

You will not be asked detailed questions on medicine. For instance, you won't be asked to explain in detail how the circulation of the blood works. Instead you will be asked about:

- important changes in medical history
- the factors that affect change
- the role of key people who have affected change
- trends and turning points
- continuity and why things stay the same
- whether change is always progress.

There are two **extension studies**, and you must study at least one of them:

- Medicine and public health from Roman Britain to c1350
- Medicine and public health c1350 to the present day.

You have probably only studied one of the two. **Make sure you answer the question on the right one**.

There is one **examination** paper, which lasts 1 hour and 15 minutes.

The exam questions will always follow the pattern below.

- The number of **marks** you can score for each question is given.
- So is the **time** the examiners recommend you spend on each question. It leaves you 5 minutes to check your answers at the end.

Question 1

4 marks 5 minutes	Question 1 will give you two sources from different times in history and ask you about changes between the two sources.

Question 2

9 marks 15 minutes	Question 2 will ask you about two important aspects of medicine. You must choose **one** aspect to write about.

Question 3 or Question 4

12 marks 20 minutes	Here you get a choice of question. Answer one or the other, but **not** both. These questions usually contain some information for you to use, and they will be about an important aspect of medicine.

Question 5 or Question 6

(a) 9 marks (b) 16 marks 30 minutes	Questions 5 and 6 will always be in 2 parts (a) and (b). You **must** answer both parts of the same question. One question is on the first extension study, and one on the second. This question will need a long written answer, and marks will be awarded for writing clear and accurate English as well as for your knowledge of history.

To help you prepare for this examination, this book does three things.

- First, it helps you with content. There is a two-page overview of the **content** of the Unit. There are also SuperFacts for each part of the Unit (SuperFacts are the key bits of information you need to answer the questions.)

- Secondly, it helps you with **questions**. It explains what you have to do to answer every type of question you will be asked and gives you a chance to test yourself.

- Thirdly, it helps you with **answers**. It provides **model answers** to all the questions, so you can see how well you did.

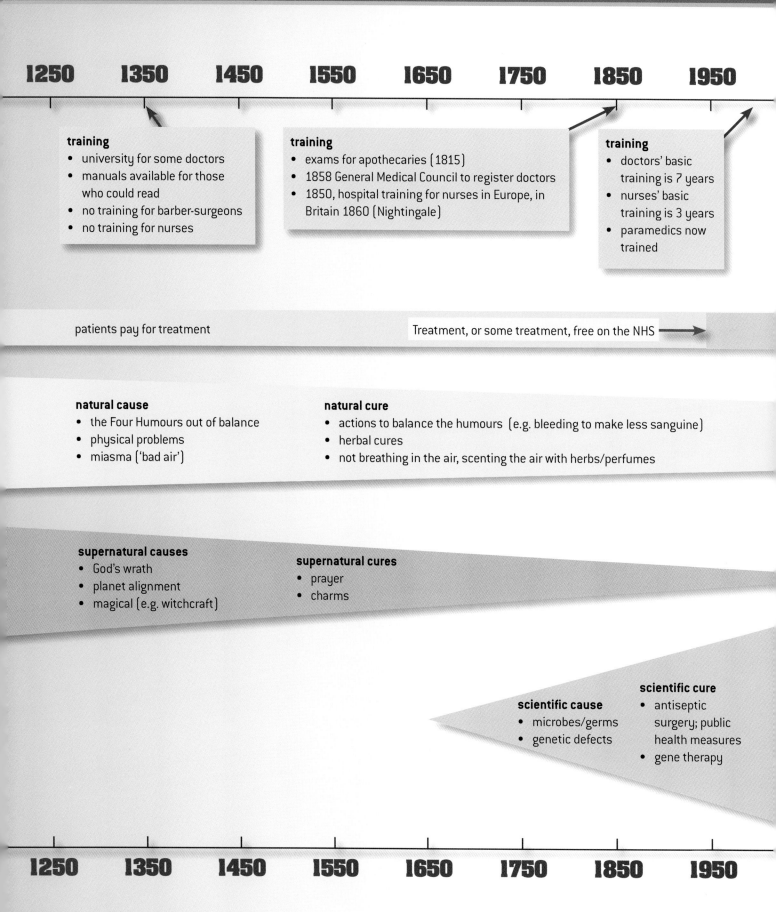

| 1250 | 1350 | 1450 | 1550 | 1650 | 1750 | 1850 | 1950 |

training
- university for some doctors
- manuals available for those who could read
- no training for barber-surgeons
- no training for nurses

training
- exams for apothecaries (1815)
- 1858 General Medical Council to register doctors
- 1850, hospital training for nurses in Europe, in Britain 1860 (Nightingale)

training
- doctors' basic training is 7 years
- nurses' basic training is 3 years
- paramedics now trained

patients pay for treatment

Treatment, or some treatment, free on the NHS

natural cause
- the Four Humours out of balance
- physical problems
- miasma ('bad air')

natural cure
- actions to balance the humours (e.g. bleeding to make less sanguine)
- herbal cures
- not breathing in the air, scenting the air with herbs/perfumes

supernatural causes
- God's wrath
- planet alignment
- magical (e.g. witchcraft)

supernatural cures
- prayer
- charms

scientific cause
- microbes/germs
- genetic defects

scientific cure
- antiseptic surgery; public health measures
- gene therapy

| 1250 | 1350 | 1450 | 1550 | 1650 | 1750 | 1850 | 1950 |

war

Examples
- practice with wounds
- Galen's surgical experience
- funding for blood clotting research, WWI
- US government funding for penicillin manufacture, WWII

government

Examples
- government healthcare provision (NHS)
- Funding for research (Human Genome Project)

science and technology

Examples
- printing (spreads ideas)
- microscopes (germs visible)
- improved equipment (MRI scanners, endoscopes)
- crystallography (found DNA)

chance

Examples
- Fleming and penicillin

CHANGE

Examples
- scientific thinking (focus on experiment in 17th century)

attitudes and beliefs

CONTINUITY

Examples
- Harvey
- Jenner
- Fleming
- Bevan
- Jenner and the link between cowpox and smallpox'

individuals

Examples
- the Church banning dissection
- universities still teaching Galen after Vesalius' book
- general public acceptance of a treatment (prayer, herbal cures)
- people not accepting vaccination
- people not accepting women doctors
- doctors not accepting NHS

Examples
- People who did not accept vaccination (the Royal Society refused to publish Jenner's work, many people refused vaccination)

Core summary

During this period, people had different ideas about the causes of disease. Many people believed in supernatural causes: that God, witches or the position of the planets sent disease. Others, however, believed in various natural causes, including an imbalance in the body's 'humours' (an idea first outlined by the Ancient Greeks) and 'bad' air.

Doctors treated disease according to their ideas about what had caused it. Supernatural diseases were treated with prayers, magical charms or offerings to the gods. Natural diseases were treated with various herbal and other cures, including 'bleeding' patients and 'purging' them by making them vomit or causing diarrhoea.

Medicine was affected by outside influences as well as ideas about disease and treatment. For some time the Christian Church banned dissection of human corpses. This prevented doctors from finding out how the human body worked. On the other hand, technological advances made during the Renaissance helped medicine. For example, the invention of printing meant more books were made more cheaply and people could spread medical ideas more easily.

SuperFacts Core Topic 1
Medicine c1350–c1750

SuperFacts are the key bits of information. Learn them and ask someone to test you.

Life expectancy in the 1350s was about 30 years in England (the rich often lived longer); now it is about 80. On average, three of every five children died in childhood: one at birth (many mothers died then too), another within the year and the third before adulthood. Most died of disease caused by poor living conditions or malnutrition. ●– p.5

Medical treatment was provided by doctors (who trained and passed exams and were expensive), apothecaries (trained in making medicines), barber-surgeons (untrained, mainly practical treatment) and local people known to be good at herbal cures. Who you went to depended on the illness and what you could pay. ●– p.10–11

Hospitals at this time were mostly places where the old were cared for by monks or nuns. Some hospitals cared for people with particular diseases such as leprosy. ●– p.10–11

The Four Humours was a theory of disease introduced by the Ancient Greeks. They believed that your body had four different liquids (blood, phlegm, yellow bile and black bile) that had to be kept in balance. If they went out of balance, this affected your health and your behaviour. ●– p.6

Galen, a Roman doctor working in the 2nd century CE, developed a 'theory of opposites' to treat a patient whose humours were out of balance. ●– p.6–7

Balancing the humours If a person had too much phlegm (linked to moisture and winter), they should eat hot, peppery food. Galen wrote many books about medicine and surgery that summed up medical ideas at the time. Galen believed in bloodletting as a treatment and a preventative measure. ●– p.6–7

The first medical school was set up in Salerno in the 10th century. Galen's books were used to train doctors, who were given no practical experience and did no further research. ●– p.7

Natural remedies (such as herbal cures) were also used by medieval doctors. Herbs were burned on the fire (or carried in metal balls called pomanders) to act against 'bad' air. Spices and stones (such as bezoar) were also ground up as medicine. ●– p.7

Some doctors blamed the planets for disease They studied the planets' movements to decide how to treat patients. *A vade mecum* was a handbook for doctors that included astrology charts and charts of different colours of urine to use for diagnosis. ●– p.7

The Black Death (also called bubonic plague) swept across Europe in the 14th century, reaching England in 1348. It was carried by fleas on black rats and got into a person's bloodstream when the flea bit them. People got a fever and had swellings in their groin and armpits that became black bruises. About a third of the population died. ●– p.8

Causes suggested for the Black Death God's punishment for human sins; a bad positioning of the planets Mars, Jupiter and Saturn; 'bad ' air (caused by dirt in the streets or the breath of those affected); plots by witches or Jews. ●– p.8–9

Cures suggested for the Black Death Prayer; burning or smelling herbs and spices; isolation; cleaning rubbish off the streets; flagellation (whipping as a penance for sins); wearing lucky charms. Many people tried several of these. None worked. ●– p.9

The Renaissance was when people rediscovered Ancient Greek and Roman ideas; testing by experiment replaced accepting information in books. The Church split into Catholic and Protestant during the Reformation and lost some authority. ◖– p.12

The Medical Renaissance was the change in medical ideas affected by Renaissance thinking and inventions that lasted into the 17th century. It was helped by printing, the weakening of Church authority and various technological inventions that came from scientific experimentation. ◖– p.12–13

Dissection of human corpses became more common as people questioned old ideas and began to investigate scientifically. Leonardo da Vinci and Vesalius made detailed drawings of the inside of the human body. Instead of using Galen's surgical instructions (based on pigs), some doctors used diagrams based on the human body. ◖– p.12

Vesalius published *Fabric of the Human Body* in 1543. Based on human dissections, it showed that Galen's surgical books were wrong about the structure of the human heart (he said the septum had holes that blood passed through; it doesn't); liver (he said it had five lobes; it has two) and lower jaw (he said it had two bones; it has one). ◖– p.12

Printing meant that many more books could be produced, faster and more cheaply, than by copying by hand. Printed medical texts (such as Vesalius' *Fabric of the Human Body*) spread medical knowledge all over Europe. This encouraged further investigations and experiments. ◖– p.12

Scientific experimentation became popular. Groups such as the Royal Society in London (whose patron was King Charles II) exchanged ideas with similar societies in other countries. These groups encouraged observation and accurate recording in all experiments, including those with medical applications. ◖– p.12

William Harvey developed his ideas about the way blood circulates around the body after learning how pumps work. In 1628, he published *An Anatomical Account of the Motion of the Heart and Blood in Animals* explaining his ideas. ◖– p.13

Better equipment (such as microscope lenses that gave bigger, clearer magnification) helped scientists. Bacteria were discovered by Antonie van Leeuwenhoek, who described these 'animalcules' to the Royal Society in London in 1673. ◖– p.13

New ideas were not always accepted Many people were reluctant to change their thinking. Harvey's book was not used in medical schools until 40 years after it was first printed; surgeons were still trained using Galen's theories. When the bubonic plague returned in 1665, many of the treatments used were the same as in 1350. ◖– p.13

New ideas were not always immediately useful Harvey's ideas about circulation were interesting, but did not directly improve thinking about the cause and treatment of disease. Most ordinary doctors did not even hear of Harvey's ideas, or Vesalius'. They continued to treat according to the Four Humours or astrology. ◖– p.13

New ideas were not always linked to disease. Van Leeuwenhoek's bacteria were seen as an example of how microscopes had improved. Nobody at the time made the link between bacteria and the causes of disease. ◖– p.13

edexcel ⁞ **key terms**

dissection Cutting up something dead, carefully, to see what is inside.

Four Humours The name given to a theory, first advanced by the Ancient Greeks, that the body is made up of four different liquids ('humours') which must be kept in balance, otherwise a person becomes ill.

miasma The word often used by medieval doctors to describe 'bad' air, which was full of bad smells, from dirt and decay to sewage.

Results**Plus**
Top tip

Knowing the theory of the Four Humours is vital to your study of medicine. Learn the chart on ◖– p.6 of the textbook. If you find it difficult to learn all four humours, learn two of them very thoroughly and always give them as your examples.

Need more help?
You can find a longer explanation of each SuperFact in your Edexcel textbook, *Schools History Project: Medicine and Surgery*. Look for this symbol ◖–, which will give you the page number.

Core summary

During this period, people's ideas about the causes of disease changed dramatically. Once the connection between germs and disease was made, scientists could work towards finding cures for diseases.

Advances in technology, combined with changing ideas about disease and a greater openness to experiment, led to scientists researching ways of preventing many epidemic diseases and other illnesses. Progress was slow, but by the end of the period there was a vaccine to prevent typhoid and vaccines against cholera and TB were being developed.

SuperFacts Core Topic 2
Medicine c1750–c1900

SuperFacts are the key bits of information. Learn them and ask someone to test you.

Life expectancy in the 1750s was, on average, about 31 in the UK (the rich, and professionals such as doctors, usually lived longer). Now the average is about 80. ● p.18

The Industrial Revolution led to the rapid expansion of crowded industrial towns – partly because factories attracted workers from rural areas where new farming methods limited jobs. However, people in towns had less access to fresh food than in the countryside. ● p.19

Working and living conditions for industrial workers were bad: long hours, in airless factories, with dangerous machines; crowded, damp, badly ventilated houses with several families to a house; sewers running into the rivers where people got their water for drinking and cooking from. ● p.19

Diphtheria, smallpox and tuberculosis (TB) were killer diseases that often broke out in epidemics and were spread by touch or droplet infection (sneezing and coughing). They spread easily in crowded factories, homes and streets. ● p.20

Cholera and typhoid were killer diseases that often broke out in epidemics and spread in bacteria found in sewage. They spread easily in places where people used water from rivers that sewers emptied into for cooking, drinking and cleaning. ● p.20

Cures suggested for cholera Prayer; cleaning the house; whitewashing walls with lime; burning the clothes and bedding of the dead person; burning barrels of tar to make smoke in the streets against the miasma; wearing lucky charms. ● p.21

Smallpox was a killer disease, but some people survived several epidemics especially if they had the disease mildly the first time. For several centuries, doctors in China had used inoculation: putting some pus from a smallpox blister into a small cut on the hand of the person being inoculated, giving them a mild version of the disease. ● p.22

Inoculation spread to Asia and Lady Mary Wortley Montague saw it used in Turkey. She had her children inoculated against smallpox in 1721 and made it fashionable. People held smallpox parties and were all inoculated together. Not everyone could afford to pay for inoculation and some doctors performed the procedure badly, so it failed. ● p.22

Edward Jenner, a Gloucestershire doctor, was told by locals that people who caught the milder disease of cowpox did not catch smallpox. In 1796, Jenner inoculated a boy called James Phipps with cowpox, then smallpox immediately after the cowpox and again months later. He tried with 23 more people, including his baby son. It worked. ● p.23

Jenner published pamphlets on his 'vaccination' system, explaining how he had experimented, how he had tested his results, and how to vaccinate. Many doctors began to vaccinate. In 1802, the Jenner Society was set up to encourage vaccination and the British government began to pay for people to have free vaccination. ● p.23

ResultsPlus
Watch out!

Be clear about the difference between these:

Inoculation used a small amount of a disease to give someone a mild form of the disease. If they then caught the disease, they had it in a milder form.

Jenner's vaccination gave people a dose of one disease (cowpox) to protect them against a more deadly one (smallpox).

Pasteur's vaccine, named in honour of Jenner's vaccination idea, used a chemically weakened version of a disease to protect against it.

A cartoon about Jenner's cowpox vaccine, published in 1802.

edexcel ⠿ key terms

culture In the context of medicine and this book, bacteria or other microorganisms grown for research.

GP 'General Practitioner', a doctor who does not specialise in a particular kind of medicine, but who treats patients locally at a surgery, passing those who need specialist treatment on to a specialist at a hospital.

microbes The name given to small particles of matter, many of which can be germs or bacteria and cause disease.

spontaneous generation The theory of disease that says that germs were the result of disease, not the cause of disease.

Opposition to Jenner, especially at first, came from people who didn't understand his ideas. Some pointed out that he could not explain why vaccination worked and that it only worked with cowpox and smallpox, not other diseases. Some doctors followed his instructions badly and their patients still caught smallpox. ●▸ p.23

Germ theory is the idea that germs, microbes in the air, cause decay (later extended to disease). Before, microbes could be seen through microscopes but were said to be the result, not the cause, of disease. Many people believed that spontaneous generation caused diseases. ●▸ p.24

Louis Pasteur published his germ theory in 1861, showing that microbes caused decay. While investigating the problem of beer and vinegar going sour in brewing, he found microbes in the sour liquids. He also found that liquids did not go sour in a sealed container (which kept away the microbes in the air) or if heated (because the heat killed the microbes). ●▸ p.24

Robert Koch tested whether bacteria caused disease as well as decay. He worked on this from 1875 with a team of researchers funded by the German government. Koch and his team identified the microbes that cause anthrax in sheep. Their work made the link between bacteria and disease clear. ●▸ p.24

Need more help?
You can find a longer explanation of each SuperFact in your Edexcel textbook, *Schools History Project: Medicine and Surgery*. Look for this symbol ●▸, which will give you the page number.

New vaccines In 1879, Pasteur's team were researching chicken cholera microbes. As part of this, they injected chickens with a culture of the bacteria. A dish of culture accidently left on one side had weakened. When it was used, the chickens didn't get the disease. Pasteur's vaccines were a weakened form of the disease. ● p.24

New bacteria Koch and his team used chemical dyes to stain bacteria so they could study them more easily under a microscope. They discovered the bacteria that caused TB (1882) and cholera (1883). ● p.24

Research teams were important to 19th century developments because a person working alone was more likely to make mistakes and teams did more work in the same time. Also, people brought different specialisms to the team and could discuss problems, check each other's work and suggest new lines of enquiry. ● p.25

Funding was important to 19th century developments because it meant researchers could afford equipment and supplies. They could afford new technology (such as more powerful microscopes). They could pay team members. People who were paid wages stayed longer, so the research lasted longer. ● p.25

Doctors had to be accepted by the Royal College of Surgeons, the Royal College of Physicians or the Society of Apothecaries before they could set up practices. After 1815, doctors licensed by the Society of Apothecaries had to pass exams. In 1858, a General Medical Council was set up to register and examine doctors. ● p.26

Dissection of dead bodies was still uncommon in 1750. Doctors were trained mostly from books, although medical schools and hospitals were allowed to dissect a small number of criminals' bodies after execution. Some medical schools and hospitals, desperate for bodies to train surgeons on, secretly bought bodies from grave robbers. ● p.26

The Anatomy Act (1832) allowed hospitals and training schools to take the bodies of people who died in the workhouse and whose bodies were not claimed by a relative. This slowed down grave robbing and made more bodies available for dissection. ● p.26

John Hunter was a surgeon who ran an anatomy school in London. He dissected; emphasised observations and experiments; published works about his dissections and also his other studies (including changes in the body in pregnancy). ● p.27

Forceps were invented in the 17th century. Midwives needed training to use them successfully. So there was a rise in the number of male midwives as midwifery was professionalised. ● p.28

Female midwives were still in demand. People who could not pay a male professional, and those who disapproved of a man helping women give birth, still used female midwives. ● p.28

Florence Nightingale took nurses to the Crimean War (1854–56) and improved hygiene there (the death rate in the hospital in Scutari fell from 42% to 2%). The newspapers reported her improvements and the public gave money for her to set up a nurse training school (1860). Her book *Notes on Nursing* (1860) was published in 11 languages. ● p.29

Elizabeth Garrett Anderson worked as a nurse; was refused training as a doctor; but went to the lectures until forced to stop. In 1865, she applied to the Society of Apothecaries (the only organisation whose rules did not ban women). With a certificate from them she could practise as a doctor. ● p.29

The Society of Apothecaries turned Anderson down. Her father sued them. The Society took her, but changed their rules to ban women in the future. ● p.29

Anderson's work Anderson set up the New Hospital for Women in 1872. In 1874, she helped to set up the London School of Medicine for Women. In 1876, an Act of Parliament made it the law that women could work as doctors. ● p.28–29

From 1877, women could train as doctors at university, but many people said women: were too emotional for dissections and operations; were not clever enough to learn the job; would never be accepted by patients. ● p.28

Medical care for the rich and professional class was given by a trained doctor, who came to the house, for a large fee. Nurses were hired if needed. Medicine was paid for. The quality and training of doctors and nurses varied. ● p.30

Medical care for the middle and working class was provided by a GP, as long as they could pay his fee. Medicine had to be paid for. Some doctors set up sick clubs, where people made regular weekly payments to cover the cost of any treatment. Otherwise, they had to go to the local hospital as an out-patient. ● p.30

Poor people who were old, sick or disabled went to the workhouse. In the 1860s, only 3,000 of the 28,550 inmates in London workhouses were able-bodied. But medical care was very basic. Louisa Twining and others campaigned for improvements. ● p.30–31

From 1867, workhouses had to have infirmaries with full-time doctors for those who couldn't work, separate from the workhouse. These were paid for by taxes, as were new hospitals for the mentally ill and people with infectious diseases. ● p.31

The first cottage hospital was built in 1859 By 1900, there were about 300. They were small local hospitals; the doctors were GPs who visited daily; nurses provided all the care. Many provided free care to local people, others charged small fees. ● p.28

Many people treated themselves They bought herbal or chemical 'preparations' from apothecaries. Pills became very popular after 1844, when William Brockedon invented a machine that made them quickly, to the same size, in large quantities. ● p.32

Some people tried 'scientific' cures, such as using magnets, hypnotism or having electrical shocks. These replaced the supernatural cures of earlier times. ● p.33

Results Plus
Watch out!

It is important to say that new discoveries were seldom an instant success, as people resisted the new ideas behind them. Also, there were some discoveries (such as Jenner's vaccination) that depended on a doctor performing the procedure properly. If the procedure failed because it was badly done, there was a danger that people would blame the procedure, not the doctor, and think the procedure did not work.

In the same way, it is important to say that the passing of a law allowing something is not enough to make that thing happen. The fact that women could register as doctors after the 1876 Act is important. However, women doctors were not instantly accepted. There was a lot of resistance to the idea and opposition from fellow students and teachers.

Need more help?
You can find a longer explanation of each SuperFact in your Edexcel textbook, *Schools History Project: Medicine and Surgery*. Look for this symbol ●, which will give you the page number.

Core summary

Since 1900, ideas about the cause of disease have been affected by scientific discoveries such as the role of DNA and genetic links to some illnesses. From the twentieth century, medical treatment became widely available for the first time. Scientific medicine became the usual option, with some people opting for alternative medical practices such as acupuncture or homeopathy.

Scientific advances have led to a better understanding of the causes of disease, as well as more high-tech methods of preventing and treating disease. Keyhole surgery and sophisticated scanning (X-ray, MRI, CAT, ultrasound) allow doctors to examine and monitor health far more carefully than was possible before.

Because technology advanced more rapidly in the twentieth century, our ability to monitor and investigate disease advanced rapidly too. Treatments and cures have still needed to be researched and tested, but the twentieth century saw a rise in the number of scientists conducting research into disease and the amount of funding available.

SuperFacts Core Topic 3
Medicine c1900–present day

SuperFacts are the key bits of information. Learn them and ask someone to test you.

Life expectancy in 1901 was, on average, about 47 in the UK (the rich, and professionals such as doctors, still usually lived longer). Now the average is about 80. This difference comes from better living standards, better diet and improvements in the understanding and treatment of disease. ● p.39

Better understanding of disease Pasteur's germ theory of 1861 had led to a greater understanding of the causes of disease. This understanding grew in the 20th century, as did the discovery of a number of vaccines to treat previously fatal illnesses such as typhoid (1896), TB (1906), diphtheria (1913) and measles (1964). ● p.40

'Magic bullets' was the term used for drugs that would cure diseases, rather than preventing them (as vaccination did). Koch laid the foundation by finding antitoxins, the chemicals the body makes to fight infection. Emil von Behring (previously on Koch's team) isolated the antitoxins against diphtheria and used them in a serum to prevent diphtheria. ● p.40

Paul Ehrlich used the knowledge that dye stained microbes (Koch) and antitoxins only attacked disease (Behring) to combine dye and chemical to make a magic bullet against syphilis. He and his team worked for many years before they found it. This was only possible because they had government funding. ● p.40

Sahachiro Hata joined Ehrlich's team in 1909. He was asked to re-test the compounds previously used and found that the 606th, which had been rejected, worked. The drug, Salvarsan 606, showed that chemical drugs could target and cure illness. ● p.40

Gerhard Domagk found the second magic bullet in 1932. He found that a red dye stopped some kinds of blood poisoning. The vital ingredient of his magic bullet was sulphonamide. This was important because other sulphonamide drugs were found to cure pneumonia, scarlet fever and meningitis. ● p.41

Alexander Fleming was a chemist at St Mary's Hospital, London. He was working on drugs to fight the bacteria that cause infection. He noticed that mould had started growing in one of his dishes of bacteria and that the germs were not growing where the mould was. ● p.42

Fleming's research into the germ-killing mould showed that it was a powerful antibiotic, which he called penicillin. In 1929, Fleming published the results of his work with penicillin, but he could not get funding to take the work further with living things. ● p.42

Howard Florey and Ernst Chain got funding to work on penicillin in Oxford in 1939. In 1940 they tested it on mice. In 1941 they gave it to a patient who was dying from infection. It worked. He started to get better, but there was only a small amount of penicillin available. When it ran out, the patient died. ● p.42

Mass-producing penicillin was slow and Florey and Chain could not get the UK or the US government to help. Then, in 1941, the USA entered the Second World War. The US government knew that many people died in wars from infection, not wounds. They funded the mass production of penicillin. ● p.43

Doctors were still paid a fee in the early 20th century. Apart from the basic care given by GPs, most doctors specialised in different kinds of illnesses and types of surgery. GPs would perform minor surgery like taking out tonsils. Nurses were hired if needed. Medicine was paid for. ●- p.44

Cottage hospitals and hospitals in cities offered basic care for the sick. There were also specialist hospitals for the mentally ill and for those with infectious diseases (such as TB). Hospitals were funded by donations so had to keep raising money. Many of them also charged for treatment. ●- p.44

The Boer War (1899–1902) Over a third of the men who volunteered to fight in this war had to be turned away because they were not fit enough. This led to a change in the government's attitude to involvement in public health. ●- p.45

Government involvement increased with laws that introduced free health visitors to visit new mothers (1907) and provision for some free medical care for some working men (the 1911 National Insurance Act: workers, employers and the government all paid into a fund that paid for treatment for the worker, but not for his family). In 1938, 3,000 children died of diphtheria. The government began a free diphtheria vaccination campaign. ●- p.45

Better training By 1900, nurses had to be trained (the Nursing Act of 1919 set up the General Nursing Council to set standards) and doctors had to have a medical degree (and be accepted by the General Medical Council). The 1902 Midwives Act said that midwives had to be trained, too. ●- p.45

The Ministry of Health (1919) showed the government taking responsibility for the nation's health. But care was still a mixture of private care, local government care and private funding of hospitals. Charges varied for care and medicine. Many people treated themselves with mixtures of their own or bought from the chemist. ●- p.45

During the Second World War (1939–45) the government took charge of many aspects of peoples' lives to run the war efficiently. The Ministry of Health ran the Emergency Medical Service that took over hospitals to provide free medical care, giving more operating theatres, equipment and ambulance and blood transfusion services. ●- p.46

The Beveridge Report (1942) was made during the Second World War. It suggested the government should provide various kinds of care for the less well-off, including a free National Health Service. ●- p.46

Aneurin Bevan, the Minister of Health, pushed through the NHS, even though many doctors opposed the idea and refused to work under it at first. It finally went into operation in 1948. ●- p.46

---

edexcel ▦ key terms

crystallography In this context, the study of the patterns created by various parts of atoms through X-rays.

DNA Deoxyribonucleic acid: the part of each cell in your body that contains its genetic instructions.

magic bullets The name given to drugs that, when in the body, target the microbes that cause disease and nothing else within the body.

stem cells Cells that can grow and divide into any of the more than 200 types of cell in the body.

Need more help?

You can find a longer explanation of each SuperFact in your Edexcel textbook, *Schools History Project: Medicine and Surgery*. Look for this symbol ●-, which will give you the page number.

The National Health Service initially provided free treatment by GPs, hospitals, dentists and opticians; ambulances and emergency treatment; free medicines or other prescriptions. This was a big change from the limited free care available before, which had never covered non-working women, children or the elderly. ● p.46

The cost of the NHS was far greater than the government had expected. It did not get smaller, as the government had hoped, as the years passed and much illness was prevented. The government had to introduce charges for prescriptions in 1951. ● p.46

Rising costs The NHS costs more and more today, mostly because of improvements in medical care. People live longer (but are more likely to develop problems that need treatment); there is a wider range of more complicated treatments and surgical procedures; there are new drugs (which are often expensive) to fight many conditions. ● p.46

Modern training means doctors spend at least seven years training, and nurses spend three. Both are expected to have practical experience as well as academic training. There is more specialisation for nurses as well as doctors. Trained paramedics now go out on emergency calls to provide quicker emergency treatment. ● p.48–49

Technology allows hospitals to investigate patients' bodies using a variety of scanners (X-rays, CAT scans, MRI scans) that all show up different parts of the body. Modern hospital monitors track patients' heart rates, blood pressure, etc., while endoscopes let doctors examine the inside of a patient without operating. ● p.53

Technology allows hospitals to treat patients using radiotherapy, laser therapy and keyhole surgery. Technology has advanced to a point where pacemakers and kidney dialysis machines keep people alive who would have died previously. ● p.53

Genetics was first studied in the 19th century. Gregor Mendel used plants to show how characteristics are passed down the generations. As technology (X-rays, electron microscopes) improved, scientists could use crystallography to study individual cells and see what they were made up of. ● p.50

DNA is found in every cell in the body. It is the set of codes for your body: your height, hair colour, eye colour, inherited conditions (such as sickle cell anaemia) and other conditions. ● p.50

Francis Crick and James Watson began investigating the structure of DNA in 1951, using X-ray crystallography from Maurice Wilkins and Rosalind Franklin of King's College Hospital, London. In 1953, one of Franklin's X-rays convinced Crick and Watson that DNA had a double helix structure. Once they knew this, they could begin to analyse DNA. ● p.50

The Human Genome Project, led by Crick, began work in 1990 to map every single gene in the human body (30,000–35,000). The project had hundreds of scientists working in 18 teams. The information was collected by 2003, but still needs analysing. Some genes that pass on inherited conditions such as sickle cell anaemia have been identified. ● p.50

Genetic research is important because it can lead to the prevention of genetic illnesses. It has also shown that stem cells can be changed into other kinds of cells; doctors in the future might be able to use this to replace faulty cells with new ones made using stem cells. ●▬ p.50

Scientific research has led to many medical advances, but it has needed publicity, funding and continued research. Sometimes, drugs could have unwanted side effects. The drug thalidomide (given to pregnant women in the 1960s to control nausea) affected the growth of the unborn babies, especially their limbs. ●▬ p.52

Blood transfusions often killed the recipient until Landsteiner found there were four blood groups: the donor and patient had to match (1901). But blood couldn't be stored until, in 1915, sodium citrate was found to stop clotting in stored blood. Blood cells still deteriorated quickly until new methods of storing blood were found (1916). ●▬ p.52

Some people try 'alternative' medicine such as using magnets, hypnotism, homeopathy or having acupuncture (long practised in China). These replaced the supernatural cures of earlier times. Some of them have been shown to work. ●▬ p.55

Technology now helps people to monitor their health at home. Diabetics can monitor their blood sugar levels with several types of 'home test'. Home testing equipment to monitor blood pressure is also available. ●▬ p.53

New types of infection, resistant to antibiotics, became a fatal problem in some hospitals in the late 20th and early 21st century. These include MRSA and *C.difficile*. So now scientists have to look for a way to fight these new infections. ●▬ p.54

Results Plus
Top tip

When asked questions about what people believed about the causes and treatment of disease, do be careful to show that you understand that not all people (in any time period) believed the same thing. Don't say: 'In the medieval period, people believed that the planets caused disease. Now they don't.' Say: 'In the medieval period, many people, including doctors, believed that the movement of the planets could cause disease. Now, few people believe this.'

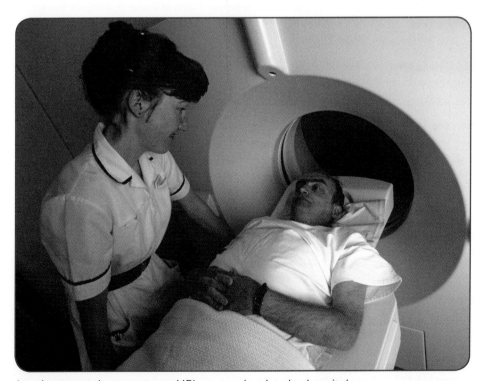

A patient preparing to enter an MRI scanner in a London hospital.

Need more help?
You can find a longer explanation of each SuperFact in your Edexcel textbook, *Schools History Project: Medicine and Surgery*. Look for this symbol ●▬, which will give you the page number.

Extension summary

When the Romans came to Britain in 43 CE, they brought their ideas about medicine, health and hygiene. They had various ideas about the causes of disease, but were sure there was a link between dirt and disease and also between 'bad' air and disease.

The Romans had a strong central government. They believed government should provide facilities such as clean water, drains, sewers, public baths and toilets. Most towns, even on the edge of the Roman Empire (such as Britain), had these facilities.

Once the Romans left, various tribes took over different parts of Britain. They let towns decline; there was no central government to provide public health facilities. Towns began to grow again in the Middle Ages, and there was a single government again, but the idea of the government being responsible for public health had gone. People still saw a link between dirt and disease, but dealt with the situation less effectively.

SuperFacts Extension Study 1
Medicine and public health from Roman Britain to c1350

SuperFacts are the key bits of information. Learn them and ask someone to test you.

The Romans conquered Britain in 43 CE, bringing their culture and ideas (including medical treatments and ideas about hygiene). They did not completely change medical thinking. After the Romans came, many people still used herbal cures and believed the gods caused illness. ●▶ p.66

Hippocrates Roman medicine used Greek ideas, especially those of Hippocrates. He believed in natural causes of and cures for disease (he thought disease was caused by the Four Humours getting out of balance). He also believed in clinical observation: study the symptoms; watch for change; treat the illness; predict change; take careful notes of the progress of the disease. ●▶ p.68

Galen developed Hippocrates' ideas, building on the Four Humours with his theory of opposites. He worked as a surgeon, did dissections (of animals) and wrote books on surgery and anatomy that were used in medical schools for hundreds of years. ●▶ p.68

Romans saw the causes of disease as: supernatural (the gods, a curse, the planets); 'bad' air in swampy or dirty places; an imbalance of the humours in the body. ●▶ p.69

Roman treatment of disease could be supernatural (making offerings to Salus, the god of health, prayers); natural (the use of herbal cures) or related to balancing the humours (e.g. bloodletting, purging). ●▶ p 69

Roman Britain did not have many doctors The head of the household did most of the treating, using remedies passed down in the family. Many of these treatments were the same all over the Roman Empire (saffron salve for sore eyes). Dioscorides published a book of herbal cures in the 2nd century CE. ●▶ p.69

The Roman army had hospitals to care for the sick and wounded. These hospitals had surgeons and general doctors. These doctors were used by Roman officials where there was an army barracks, but they did not treat ordinary people. ●▶ p.69

Romans believed in keeping clean, using clean water and avoiding swampy places and 'bad' air. This was based on their observations that dirt and unhealthy places were linked to disease, although they did not know what the link was. ●▶ p.70–71

Roman public baths charged a fee. Some were cheap and basic, others expensive and luxurious. All provided at least a changing room, an exercise hall, a warm room, a hot pool and a cold pool. Romans did not use soap; they oiled themselves then scraped off the oil and dirt with a strigil (a metal scraper). ●▶ p.71

Wealthy Romans had private baths attached to their homes for the family and visitors to use. However, many men still visited the public baths because they were meeting places as well as somewhere to get clean. ●▶ p.70

Roman towns had public toilets with running water which drained away into sewers or, in less important and wealthy towns, open drains. Sewage was kept separate from fresh water, even if drains were not covered. ●▶ p.70

Roman towns had fresh water piped from a clean water supply. Towns had street fountains or wells where people could collect water. Water carriers also sold it. ●▶ p.70

ResultsPlus
Watch out!

When you answer Questions 5a and 5b, you will need to be thinking about the SuperFacts from this section **AND** from the first part of the core unit *Medicine and treatment c1350–c1750.*

Treatment of disease did not change much in Europe after the Romans. There was still a mixture of supernatural, influence of planets and gods (although now disease was sent by the Christian God, not the earlier gods); natural medicine; and the Four Humours. Galen was still influential. ●- p.72–73

After the Romans, public health provision declined. Some people still saw a link between dirt and disease, but the government did not provide clean water, toilets and baths as the Romans had. ●- p.76

The Christian Church became increasingly powerful in the Middle Ages. It encouraged the idea that disease was God's punishment and that prayer and pilgrimage would bring a cure. It discouraged dissection of human bodies, and approved of the work of Galen. However, it did encourage monks and nuns to care for the sick. ●- p.72–73

Roman doctors did not have to be trained, although many doctors in the Roman world were, in fact, Greek and had trained in Alexandria, Egypt (where human dissection was allowed). Most doctors learned by working with an experienced doctor and/or reading some of Hippocrates' books (his ideas written down by followers). ●- p.74

In the early Middle Ages, doctors did not have to be trained but some monasteries had important collections of medical books and became centres of learning. Some of these developed into universities that offered some medical training as part of a ten-year degree. ●- p.74

By the 12th century there were medical schools training doctors. Medical training was based on a collection of books called the *Ars Medicinae* (Art of Medicine), which included the works of Galen and some works written by Muslim authors. By the 13th century, most towns wanted proof of study to allow a doctor to practise there. ●- p.75

Medieval cities were dirty People threw rubbish and sewage into the streets, or into the same rivers where their water for drinking and cooking came from. There was no centralised government (as in Roman times), so when laws about cleaning up rubbish were passed – often when disease broke out – they were not properly enforced. ●- p.76

By the end of the Middle Ages, well-off people often left money in their will to pave the streets or improve the water supply of towns. Some cities had 'stewes', large bathhouses, where people bathed in big wooden tubs. Wealthier people had their own baths and privies (toilets). ●- p.77

Hospitals in the Middle Ages Monks and nuns gave some medical care; this grew from the custom of giving travellers food and a bed for the night. However, their care was as much spiritual help as medical treatment. ●- p.77

There were over 1000 hospitals in Britain by the end of the Middle Ages, most of them (such as St Bartholomew's, London, established 1123) funded by donations. Almshouses to care for the old and poor were also set up by donation. Specialist 'houses' were set up for particular infectious illnesses (such as lazar houses for lepers). ●- p.78

edexcel ::: key terms

hospital The word 'hospital' has changed meaning over time. A Roman hospital was a place where the sick were treated by doctors. A medieval hospital was a place where the poor, sick and old were looked after by monks or nuns.

pilgrimage A pilgrimage is a journey to a place that is holy or important in a particular religion to pray to a god, saint or person who is linked to that place. Some places were particularly linked to praying for health or cures.

Need more help?
You can find a longer explanation of each SuperFact in your Edexcel textbook, *Schools History Project: Medicine and Surgery*. Look for this symbol ●-, which will give you the page number.

Extension summary

Between the medieval period and the present day, attitudes to public health provision changed dramatically. The belief that the government had no right to interfere in public health issues gave way to the belief that the government was responsible not only for public health works (for example, providing drains, sewers and rubbish collection) but also for providing a health service for its citizens.

The nineteenth century saw a sharp rise in infectious diseases (such as cholera and TB) caused by the poor living and working conditions in the rapidly growing industrial towns. By the end of the century, the government had begun to pass laws to improve the provision of fresh water and drainage.

SuperFacts Extension Study 2
Public health from c1350 to the present day

SuperFacts are the key bits of information. Learn them and ask someone to test you.

Towns grew in the Middle Ages and sewage and rubbish disposal problems grew too. Some people saw a connection between dirt and disease, but many people still dumped rubbish and sewage into the street or the river they took drinking water from. ●- p.88

Town councils passed laws about cleaning the streets but, in most places, people had to pay for rubbish removal and cesspit clearance. No one expected government to pass public health laws. Some town councils raised money for drains, rubbish collection and piped water. A few towns had public baths and/or toilets. ●- p.88

Clean water was piped to London from about 1300 from the River Tyburn, north of the city. Over the years, more pipes and conduits (where water could be collected) were added. Water carriers sold it door-to-door. ●- p.89

The government tried to stop the 1665 plague from spreading. London theatres were closed and other large gatherings banned. Barrels of tar were burned in the streets. Houses where there was plague were shut up and a red cross painted on the door. The dead were collected daily on carts and buried in mass graves. ●- p.90

The government passed public health laws, although enforcement was a problem. In 1750, it raised the price of gin, saying cheap gin caused disease and death and stopped workers working well. It made smallpox vaccination compulsory in 1852 and ordered a register of those vaccinated to be kept from 1871. ●- p.91

Cholera killed thousands in 1831 It was new to Britain and spread in dirty water. As industrial towns grew rapidly (Glasgow from 77,000 in 1801 to 329,000 in 1851; Leeds from 53,000 in 1802 to 172,000 in 1851), disease spread, especially in crowded slums with poor or no sanitation. The poor, weak from malnutrition, caught TB, typhoid and cholera easily. ●- p.92

Edwin Chadwick was a member of the Poor Law Commission in charge of workhouses. In 1842 he released a report, *The Sanitary Conditions of the Labouring Population*, investigating cholera outbreaks. ●- p.93

Chadwick's report said that people needed clean water and the removal of sewage and rubbish to stay healthy and that taxes should be used for better housing, not workhouses. He had some support from newspapers, which publicised his ideas, and from some MPs. ●- p.93

Opponents to Chadwick's ideas Those who believed in *laissez faire*; the water companies, who thought they would lose money; well-off people who paid local taxes, who did not want their money spent on improving the homes of the poor. ●- p.93

The 1848 Public Health Act was passed after a bad outbreak of cholera earlier that year. It set up a General Board of Health to work until 1858. Towns could (but did not have to) set up a Board of Health, a town medical officer, sewers and rubbish removal. ●- p.93

The link between cholera and dirty water was proved by Dr John Snow in the 1854 cholera outbreak. He mapped deaths in Soho, London. Many of the dead had used the Broad Street water pump. Snow had the pump handle removed. The death rate dropped. He made links between different water companies and deaths, too. ●- p.94

Results Plus
Top tip

'The Middle Ages' and 'medieval' are both used by historians to refer to the period between the departure of the Romans and the start of the Renaissance in the late 15th century. You can use either. Be sure to capitalise **M**iddle **A**ges but, if you use it, **not** to capitalise 'medieval'.

Mounting evidence about dirt and disease After 1850, John Snow's cholera research, Louis Pasteur's germ theory (1861) and government studies that showed cities and towns had higher death rates than the countryside all caused the government to act. They began plans for sewers and water provision. ●- p.24–25, 94

In the 'Great Stink' of 1858, the water level in the Thames dropped very low in the summer. The sun heated the sewage left on the bank. The river smelt so bad that, even with disinfectant-soaked sheets over the windows, Parliament could not meet. ●- p.95

Sewers were built rapidly after the Great Stink, following plans drawn up by Joseph Bazalgette. It took seven years to complete but, by 1865, London had 1,300 miles of sewers, many of which still serve central London today. ●- p.95

The Sanitary Act of 1866 followed another cholera outbreak. It required local councils to appoint inspectors to check the water supply and drains of towns. ●- p.95

The 1875 Artisans' Dwellings Act gave town councils the right to buy up slum housing, knock it down and build better homes. It did not force them to. Few did, although some town councils did this even before the act (Birmingham did in 1870). ●- p.95

The 1875 Public Health Act said towns must have a Board of Health and a medical officer. Towns had to provide clean water, paved streets, sewers and rubbish removal. They had to check food shops to make sure the food being sold was fit to eat. ●- p.95

The Welfare State began in the 1900s, when the government abandoned *laissez faire* ideas and began to make provision for the poor, the old and the unemployed. It also began to make medical provision, such as the Schools' Medical Service and health visitors to visit mothers with babies and young children. ●- p.96

Free healthcare for some of the unemployed came under the 1911 National Insurance Act. The government, workers and employers (in some industries) paid into a fund that paid the worker sick pay or unemployment benefit for a set period of weeks and gave free medicines. Medical care did not extent to the worker's family. ●- p.96

The Ministry of Health (1919) provided free healthcare in emergencies (such as the flu epidemic that raged in 1919). It set up baby clinics to provide free vaccinations and cheap baby food, and brought many hospitals under local government control. By 1931, average British life expectancy was 58 for men and 62 for women. ●- p.96

The National Health Service (NHS, 1948) was set up by Minister of Health Aneurin Bevan, despite resistance from doctors, who feared they would not be able to make a living. The NHS provided free healthcare for everyone, including dentistry and eye care, but had to charge for prescriptions, then eye care as costs rose. ●- p.46–47, 98

Preventative measures since 1949 included more vaccines (polio, 1952; cervical cancer, 2008), government legislation to reduce pollution (the 1956 Clean Air Act) and health education (anti-smoking campaigns from the late 1960s on). ●- p.98

---

edexcel ⠿ key terms

cesspit A pit dug for sewage, either under toilets or at a central point for people to empty sewage into.

laissez faire The idea that government should not interfere in people's lives, either to regulate business or to improve living conditions.

workhouse A place where the unemployed, poor and homeless could go for very basic food and a place to sleep. Families were separated and work, such as breaking up stones, was provided.

ResultsPlus
Watch out!

When you answer Questions 6a and 6b, you will need to be thinking about the SuperFacts from this section **and** from the core unit *Medicine and treatment c1750–c1900*. The SuperFacts for this section sometimes have page number references to this section and to earlier pages of this book.

Need more help?
You can find a longer explanation of each SuperFact in your Edexcel textbook, *Schools History Project: Medicine and Surgery*. Look for this symbol ●-, which will give you the page number.

Key people

Sometimes the examiner will ask you to use information about key people in the history of medicine. For example, Question 2 may ask you about the importance of certain people in changing or improving things.

These pages help you by giving you:

- key people: names and dates
- reasons why they were important
- steps they took towards an advance
- examples of their work you can use to support the view that they were important
- links to further detail in the textbook.

Hippocrates: 4th century BCE
➤ p.6, 68, 74

- **Stressed rational, physical causes of illness, not magical or religious ones**
  e.g. He taught clinical observation, watching heartbeat, temperature, urine, etc., before deciding treatment.

- **Spread the Theory of the Four Humours**
  e.g. He taught illness could be cured by getting the humours back in balance.

- **Developed the idea of a medical profession**
  e.g. a code of conduct.

- **Ideas influenced medicine for centuries**
  e.g. works called the *Hippocratic Books*.

Galen: c160CE
➤ p.6–7, 10, 66, 68, 72, 73, 74, 75

- **Spread the Theory of the Four Humours**
  e.g. He promoted bloodletting, to cure and prevent various illnesses.
  e.g. He introduced the theory of opposites, to restore the Four Humours.

- **Influenced medicine for centuries**
  e.g. His books were used in universities for over a thousand years.

William Harvey: 1578–1657
➤ p.12–13

- **Improved knowledge of the human body**
  e.g. Published research in works like *An Anatomical Account of the Motion of the Heart and Blood in Animals*, 1628.
  e.g. Showed blood circulates repeatedly around the body, pumped by the heart.

- **Challenged ideas from the past**
  e.g. Showed Galen was wrong to say blood was made in the liver and used up in the body.

Vesalius: 1514–64
➤ p.12

- **Research based on scientific methods**
  e.g. *The Fabric of the Human Body* (1543), based on dissection of human corpses, not animals.

- **Encouraged people to challenge old ideas**
  e.g. Showed Galen was wrong to say the human septum had holes.

John Hunter: 1728–93 (pictured)
➤ p.27

- **Improved the quality of medical training**
  e.g. Demonstrated dissection to students. Encouraged careful observation and research.

- **Discovered information about disease**
  e.g. Published research into pregnancy, arthritis and sexual diseases.

Edward Jenner: 1749–1823
● p.22–23

- **Showed vaccination prevented smallpox**
  In 1796, infected 8-year-old with cowpox.
  Later repeated experiment on 23 others.

- **Encouraged further progress**
  e.g. Published research in pamphlets for others to read and check.
  e.g. Set up the Jennerian Society in London (1802) to promote vaccination.

Edwin Chadwick: 1800–90
● p.92–93

- **Following cholera outbreak, campaigned for improved living conditions for the poor**
  e.g. *Sanitary Conditions of the Labouring Population* (1842) said local taxes should be used to improve housing and hygiene.
  e.g. Campaigned for better water, sewers and rubbish disposal.

- **Helped to change attitudes towards public health**
  General Board of Health set up 1848.
  Started to undermine faith in *laissez faire*; this later led to reforms like the Public Health Act 1875.

John Snow: 1813–58
● p.94

- **Linked London cholera deaths to bad water**
  Mapped illness in 1854 cholera outbreak.
  Showed link to Broad Street water pump.

Elizabeth Garrett Anderson, 1836–1917
● p.28

- **Improved women's access to medical professions**
  Took Society of Apothecaries to court (with her father's help) to get registered as a doctor in 1865.
  Set up a medical practice in London.
  Gained medical degree in Paris.
  Set up London School of Medicine for Women in 1874
  In 1876, British government passed an act so women could enter medical professions.

ResultsPlus
Top tip

Factors inhibiting change
It sometimes took a while for people's new ideas to turn into improvements. This was not their fault. Many factors could slow down change:
- e.g. People feared the effects of Jenner's cowpox vaccinations. Then some doctors did vaccinations badly and they didn't work. It was 80 years before compulsory public vaccinations were enforced.
- e.g. Chadwick's idea to provide clean water and proper sewers for London's poor met with opposition at first. It clashed with *laissez faire* ideas and was opposed by the water companies and taxpayers (who did not want to pay the cost). It was 30 years before London got a better sewerage system.

Florence Nightingale: 1820–1910 (pictured)
● p.28

- **Demonstrated a link between cleanliness and patient recovery**
  Led team of nurses at military hospital at Scutari in the Crimean War (1854–6)
  Improved nursing care and hygiene; death rate in Scutari hospital fell from 42% to 2%.
  Success widely reported in the press.

- **Improved the quality of nursing and hospital care**
  Helped to found the Nightingale School for Nurses (1860).
  Helped start training school for midwives at King's College Hospital.
  Published *Notes on Nursing*, giving practical guidelines.
  Wrote over 200 books about hospital design and organisation.

Louis Pasteur: 1822–95
● p.24–25

- **Proved decay caused by germs in the air**
  Found bacteria that turned beer sour.
  Showed these germs came from the air.
  In 1861 published germ theory.

- **Led the way to safer surgery**
  Led surgeons, such as Lister, to see that germs from the air infected wounds.

- **Found a way to produce new vaccines**
  In 1879, accidently produced a weak strain of chicken cholera.
  Found that giving animals this weak strain prevented the disease.

ResultsPlus
Top tip

Factors helping change
As you read about the ways in which the people on these pages helped medical progress, take note of the times when the following factors helped to speed up change:
- research using scientific methods
- research published for others to share
- improved technology
- multi-disciplinary teamwork
- government funding
- war
- chance.

Robert Koch: 1843–1910
● p.24, 40

- **Used Pasteur's germ theory to find specific germs which caused killer diseases**
  e.g. Identified microbes which caused TB (1882) and cholera (1883).

- **Found ways to stain specific bacteria to aid study**
  e.g. Used chemical dyes to stain specific bacteria. This helped other scientists to study them and find vaccines.

Emil von Behring: 1854–1917
● p.40

- **Publicised the importance of antibodies**
  e.g. Used work of Pasteur and Koch to identify diphtheria antibodies:
  - these antibodies were produced by the body to try to fight off diphtheria
  - like a natural 'magic bullet', these antibodies only killed the diphtheria germs, nothing else.
  e.g. Injected diphtheria antibodies into people to protect them against the disease.

Paul Ehrlich: 1854–1917
● p.40

- **Started the search for a chemical cure for syphilis**
  Combined the work of Koch (isolating specific bacteria with dyes) and von Behring (antibodies targeting specific bacteria) to search for a chemical 'magic bullet' against specific bacteria. Research stretched on for several years, only possible because of government funding.

Sahachiro Hata: 1873–1938
● p.40

- **Found the chemical cure for syphilis**
  Joined Ehrlich's team in 1909 and checked earlier work.
  Found that compound number 606 actually did kill the syphilis germs.
  This was the first chemical 'magic bullet' – a manufactured drug that would kill only the target germs.

Gerhard Domagk: 1895–1964
● p.41

- **Produced Prontosil, the 2nd magic bullet**
  e.g. In 1932, he produced a chemical compound called a sulphonamide:
  - this acted like a magic bullet to kill germs which caused blood poisoning
  - manufactured as Prontosil; it saved thousands of lives.

- **Led the way to other sulphonamides**
  Later, sulphonamides were made which cured a range of diseases, like pneumonia.

Alexander Fleming: 1881–1955 (pictured)
p. 42–43

- **Isolated and publicised an antibiotic which could fight many diseases**
  In 1928, noticed that penicillin, in a mould on a Petri dish, killed the bacteria there.
  In 1929, published findings.

- **Unable to fund development of penicillin, but other scientists did.**

Howard Florey and Ernst Chain, 1940s
p.42–43

- **Proved effectiveness of penicillin**
  In 1939, set up team of researchers.
  In 1940, tested penicillin on mice.
  In 1941, tested it on a patient and proved that it could cure many infections.

- **Mass-produced penicillin**
  Persuaded US government to fund research into mass production. In 1944, first mass production of penicillin.

Aneurin Bevan: 1897–1960
p.46–47

- **Set up the National Health Service, despite opposition to provide:**
  free access to a GP and hospitals
  free treatment by dentists and opticians
  free health care for elderly, children and pregnant women
  free ambulances and emergency treatment.

- **Factors that stood in the way of this change**
  doctors who feared fall in income
  doctors who didn't want to work for the government
  people who worried about the cost
  people who worried about the increase in government control over society.

- **Factors that encouraged this change**
  the Beveridge Report
  medical improvements, which meant that so much more could be done for people
  people had become used to government controlling more aspects of their lives – especially during wartime
  by 1948 Bevan was Minister for Health.

Francis Crick: 1916–2004
James Watson: 1928–Present
Maurice Wilkins: 1916–2004
Rosalind Franklin: 1920–58
p.50–51, 56–57

- **Worked out the structure of DNA**
  In 1951, Watson (a chemist) and Crick (a physicist) began work at Cambridge University to discover the structure of DNA.
  Wilkins and Franklin photographed cells using X-rays.
  In 1953, Watson and Crick published a model of human DNA, showing its double helix structure.

- **Improved understanding of genetically inherited diseases**
  In 1990, Watson led the Human Genome Project to map every single gene in the human body. This increased understanding of genetically inherited diseases.

- **Paved the way for new cures and treatments**
  Scientists are currently researching ways to use gene therapy to cure illnesses such as breast cancer.

Answering questions: Question 1

What you need to do

Question 1 will always ask *What can you learn from Sources A and B about changes in ... [something]?*

The best answers:

- make **inferences** about changes from the sources [see *Top tip box*]
- and **support** those inferences with detail from both sources.

The examination paper will contain **two sources**, set out like this.

Study Sources A and B.

Source A: A cure for toothache, written down by John of Gaddesden, a leading English doctor, c1280–1361.

> Write these words on the jaw of the patient: *'In the name of the Father, Son and Holy Ghost, Amen.'* The pain will cease at once as I have often seen.

Source B: Louis Pasteur, studying illnesses in his laboratory in about 1880.

The examination paper will then ask you to answer a question like the ones below.

> *What can you learn from Sources A and B about changes in the way doctors think about the causes of illness? Explain your answer using these sources.*

or

> *What can you learn from Sources A and B about changes in the way doctors think illness should be cured? Explain your answer using these sources.*

Top tip

An **inference** is a judgement that can be made by studying the source, but is not directly stated by it.

A **supported** inference is one that uses detail from the source to prove the inference.

Consider this example:

Source A: 'The furious head teacher told Jimmy that his behaviour was disgraceful and that he had broken several school rules.'

Question: What does Source A tell us about Jimmy?

Information: *Source A tells us Jimmy broke several school rules.* [This is directly stated in the source, so it's not an inference.]

An inference could be: *Source A tells me that Jimmy is in serious trouble and is likely to be punished.* [The source does not directly tell us this, but we can infer that it is likely.]

A supported inference could be: *Source A tells me Jimmy is in serious trouble and likely to be punished. I can infer this because Jimmy broke several school rules and the head teacher was furious.* [This is an inference, with details quoted from the source to support it.]

How you do it

Let's practise. Use Sources A and B on the previous page.

What can you learn from Sources A and B about changes in the way doctors think about the causes of illness? Explain your answer using these sources.

A good answer could look like this.

Inference	Supporting detail
One thing I can infer from the two sources about changing views of the cause of illness is that doctors used to believe in religious causes of illness. Over recent centuries, this has changed. They now believe in scientific causes of illness.	I can infer this from the two sources because in Source A Gaddesden says he can cure toothache by writing religious words on the patient's jaw. I can infer from this that he thinks toothache is caused by God. But Source B shows Pasteur studying illnesses with a microscope and other scientific equipment. This shows that he must think there is a scientific explanation for illness. This is a change in how doctors thought illness was caused.

ResultsPlus
Top tip

The examiner will give you two sources and expect you to use both of them. To reach the top level, you **must** make inferences from both sources.

An answer like this, with:

- an **inference** about the **changes** asked about in the question
- supported by **detail** from **both** sources

would reach the top level.

Now test yourself

Now you practise, using the same sources.

What can you learn from Sources A and B about changes in the way doctors think illness should be cured? Explain your answer using these sources.

Inference	Supporting detail
One thing I can infer from the two sources about changing views on how illness should be cured... (i)	I can learn this from the two sources because in... (ii)

The answer
You can find suggested answers to the tasks numbered (i), (ii), etc., on page 42.

Answering questions: Question 2

What you need to do

Question 2 will give you two examples of:

*   people
*   groups of people
*   events
*   ideas
*   changes
*   continuity
*   developments

It will then ask you to choose **one** of the two examples given and explain why it (or they) changed something, improved it, or caused it to stay the same. For example:

The boxes below show two important people in the history of medicine.
Choose <u>one</u> person and explain why he or she was important in improving the treatment of illness.

| Louis Pasteur and germ theory | Florence Nightingale and the Crimean War |

The best answers will:

*   **not** just write all they know about the person or the improvement.

They will link:

*   what the **person** did
*   with the **improvement**.

So, you could think of your answer as looking like this.

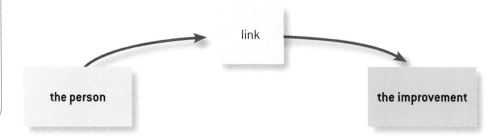

How you do it
Study this answer for Florence Nightingale. We have based it on the SuperFact on the previous page.

The person	Improvement in treatment of illness
Florence Nightingale was important in improving the treatment of illness. She took nurses to the Crimean War (1854–56) and improved hygiene in Scutari hospital. The death rate there fell from 42% to 2%.	This work improved the treatment of illness because it showed everyone the link between hygiene and illness. Newspapers reported her work, so it became widely known. The public gave money for her to set up a nurse training school in 1860, so many nurses spread her methods. Her book, called <u>Notes on Nursing</u>, was published in 11 languages, which spread her improvements abroad. All this meant that Florence Nightingale's work in the Crimea improved the treatment of illness.

Now you use the SuperFacts on this page to write an answer about Louis Pasteur, below.

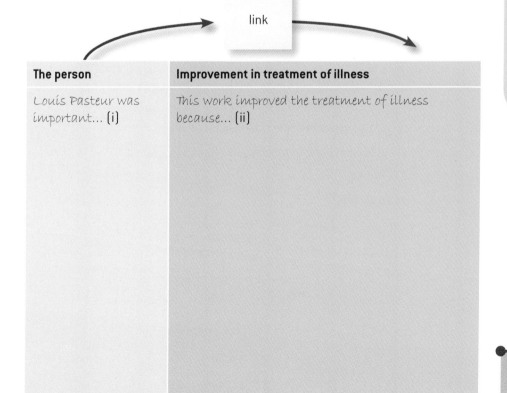

The person	Improvement in treatment of illness
Louis Pasteur was important... (i)	This work improved the treatment of illness because... (ii)

An answer like this, with **detailed information** to show the **link(s)** between the person and the improvement, will reach the top level.

SuperFacts

Germ theory is the idea that germs, microbes in the air, cause decay (later extended to disease). Before, microbes could be seen through microscopes but were said to be the result, not the cause, of disease. Many people believed that spontaneous generation caused diseases.

Louis Pasteur published his germ theory in 1861, showing that microbes caused decay. While investigating the problem of beer and vinegar going sour in brewing, he found microbes in the sour liquids. He also found that liquids did not go sour in a sealed container (which kept away the microbes in the air) or if heated (because the heat killed the microbes).

Better understanding of disease
Pasteur's germ theory of 1861 had led to a greater understanding of the causes of disease. This understanding grew in the 20th century, as did the discovery of a number of vaccines to treat previously fatal illnesses such as typhoid (1896), TB (1906), diphtheria (1913) and measles (1964).

The answer
You can find suggested answers to the tasks numbered (i), (ii), etc., on page 42.

ResultsPlus
Top tip

Questions 3 and 4 will always be followed by some useful information to help you with your answer. This extra information could be useful information, a quote or a picture.

It will be useful and relevant information. You can use other information as long as it is **relevant to the focus of the question**. You do not need to do so. Answers that are closely tied to the focus of the question, rather than talking around it, will reach the top level.

SuperFacts

Dissection of human corpses became more common as people questioned old ideas and began to investigate scientifically. Leonardo da Vinci and Vesalius made detailed drawings of the inside of the human body. Instead of using Galen's surgical instructions (based on pigs), some doctors used diagrams based on the human body.

Vesalius published *Fabric of the Human Body* in 1543. Based on human dissections, it showed that Galen's surgical books were wrong about the structure of the human heart (he said the septum had holes that blood passed through; it doesn't); liver (he said it had five lobes; it has two) and lower jaw (he said it had two bones; it has one).

Printing meant that many more books could be produced, faster and more cheaply, than by copying by hand. Printed medical texts (such as Vesalius' *Fabric of the Human Body*) spread medical knowledge all over Europe. This encouraged further investigations and experiments.

Answering questions: Questions 3 and 4

What you need to do
In the exam, you must answer **either** Question 3 or Question 4.

Questions 3 and 4 will ask you to **analyse** something. For example:

- *Why did [somebody] do [something]?*
- *In what ways did [something] help [something else] to happen?*
- *How important was the role of [somebody]?*

The questions will always give you some information to help you with your answer. For example:

Why was there so much new medical knowledge discovered during the 16th and 17th centuries?

> The following information may help you with your answer.
> During the 16th and 17th centuries there was a Medical Renaissance.
> It was a time when there was more scientific experimentation, more dissection and more scientific equipment to help research.

The best answers will show they **understand the focus** of the question and will provide **accurate and relevant information** to support their points.

How you do it
Take the question above as an example. Use the SuperFacts on the left.

- Think about why there was new medical knowledge discovered in the 16th and 17th centuries. This is the focus of the question.

- The best answers will give more than one reason, supported by accurate information. However, even one reason will get you to the top level **as long as** it has accurate and relevant supporting information.

So, each time you give a reason, take the time to support it first.

You could take a reason from the information in the box and explain it.

One reason for the growth in medical knowledge was the increase in scientific experimentation.

Scientific experimentation was done by groups such as the Royal Society in London. They exchanged ideas with each other, and with other people and groups from other countries. The idea of experimenting and exchanging ideas rather than just following a textbook means people found more out.

Now test yourself

We have used the first part of the information box to start the answer.

Finish the answer, using the rest of the information.

> Another reason why medical knowledge grew was the increase in dissection.
>
> This increased medical knowledge because ... (i)

Results Plus
Top tip

In our example, we have stressed the importance of the focus of the question. Only relevant information will reach the top level. The question we have used focuses on the harm done to people's health by the growth of industrial towns. You have to show how the growth affected health. **Don't** say, *'Industrial towns grew rapidly during the Industrial Revolution. This affected people's health'.* Give the examiner **details** about how health was affected, as we did in our examples.

> A third reason for medical knowledge growing was that people began to think about the body differently.
>
> This increased medical knowledge because ... (ii)

Remember, you can add your **own reasons**, as long as they are relevant to the focus of the question.

For example, in answer to this question, you could say:

> Another reason why medical knowledge grew was the availability of printing.
>
> This increased medical knowledge because ... (iii)

An answer like this, with **at least one** reason why medical knowledge grew and **each** explained by **supporting detail**, will reach the top level.

The answer
You can find suggested answers to the tasks numbered (i), (ii), etc., on page 42.

ResultsPlus
Top tip

In the exam, students must answer both parts of either Question 5 or Question 6. If they answer one part from Question 5 and one part from Question 6, **only one part will be marked**.

Students who have studied the extension study *Medicine and public health from Roman Britain to 1350* should answer Questions 5 (a) and (b).

Students who have studied the extension study *Public Health c1350 to present day* should answer Questions 6 (a) and (b).

SuperFacts

Romans saw the causes of disease as: supernatural (the gods, a curse, the planets); 'bad' air in swampy or dirty places; an imbalance of the humours in the body.

Roman treatment of disease could be supernatural (making offerings to Salus, the god of health, prayers); natural (the use of herbal cures) or related to balancing the humours (e.g. bloodletting, purging).

Treatment of disease did not change much in Europe after the Romans. There was still a mixture of supernatural, influence of planets and gods (although now disease was sent by the Christian God, not the earlier gods); natural medicine; and the Four Humours. Galen was still influential.

The Christian Church became increasingly powerful in the Middle Ages. It encouraged the idea that disease was God's punishment and that prayer and pilgrimage would bring a cure. It discouraged dissection of human bodies, and approved of the work of Galen. However, it did encourage monks and nuns to care for the sick.

Answering questions: Question 5 (a)

What you need to do
In the exam, you must answer **either** both parts of Question 5 **or** both parts of Question 6.

Question 5 (a) will ask you to **describe** or **explain** something. For example:

- *How did religious beliefs influence medicine from Roman times to 1350?*
- *In what ways did the Romans use hygiene to avoid illness?*
- *Explain how the key features of doctors' training changed between Roman times and c1350.*

Take the first question above as an example. The best answers to this question will:

- state **examples** of religious beliefs about medicine at this time
- use **detailed information** to explain how these beliefs influenced medicine.

How you do it
A good answer to this question might start like this.

> One way religious beliefs affected medicine was how people explained the causes of illness.

> The Romans believed in some natural causes of illness, like dirt or unbalanced humours. But they also believed in religious causes – illness caused by the gods. In medieval times, Christians still believed that some illnesses were sent by God.

The rest of the answer could be organised as below.

Using the SuperFacts on this page, put **one** fact into each box. One fact is enough for this exercise, but you should use more than one fact in the exam.

> Another way religious beliefs affected medicine was how people thought illness could be cured.

> They thought illness could be cured by... (i)

> Another way religious beliefs affected medicine was how the Church influenced medical study.

> The Church's influence can be shown because... (ii)

Listing a number of **ways** religion affected medical beliefs and giving **details** to explain **how** it did so will reach the top level.

Now test yourself

Practise a full examination answer. Write in each of the boxes to complete the answer.

Use the SuperFacts on the right to help you.

In what ways did the Romans use hygiene to avoid illness?

One way the Romans used hygiene to avoid illness was bathing.

(iii)

Another way the Romans used hygiene to avoid illness was public toilets.

(iv)

Another way the Romans used hygiene to avoid illness was by... (v)

(vi)

SuperFacts

Romans believed in keeping clean, using clean water and avoiding swampy places and 'bad' air. This was based on their observations that dirt and unhealthy places were linked to disease, although they did not know what the link was.

Roman public baths charged a fee. Some were cheap and basic, others expensive and luxurious. All provided at least a changing room, an exercise hall, a warm room, a hot pool and a cold pool. Romans did not use soap; they oiled themselves then scraped off the oil and dirt with a strigil (a metal scraper).

Wealthy Romans had private baths attached to their homes for the family and visitors to use. However, many men still visited the public baths because they were meeting places as well as somewhere to get clean.

Roman towns had public toilets with running water which drained away into sewers or, in less important and wealthy towns, open drains. Sewage was kept separate from fresh water, even if drains were not covered.

Roman towns had fresh water piped from a clean water supply. Towns had street fountains or wells where people could collect water. Water carriers also sold it.

Results Plus
Top tip

Make sure that the information you use is **relevant to the focus of the question**. Don't just say *'The Romans had public toilets with drains to take away the sewage.'* Only answers that explain **how this helped to prevent illness** will reach the top level.

The answer

You can find suggested answers to the tasks numbered (i), (ii), etc., on page 42.

Question 5 (b) will not always follow the same pattern, But, although the question types may be different, each type of question expects you to:

- use factual information to support and contradict the basic idea in the question
- come to your own overall judgement about the answer.

The question might ask:

- about how far something changed or stayed the same
- if you agree with a statement
- how different things were
- about causes or effects.

Top level answers always reach a conclusion about why, how far or whether they agree with a statement. If the question asks about the causes or effects, the best answers will show how causes or effects are linked and will weigh up the importance of each one.

SuperFacts

Roman treatment of disease could be supernatural (making offerings to Salus, the god of health, prayers); natural (the use of herbal cures) or related to balancing the humours (e.g. bloodletting, purging).

Treatment of disease did not change much in Europe after the Romans. There was still a mixture of supernatural, influence of planets and gods (although now disease was sent by the Christian God, not the earlier gods); natural medicine; and the Four Humours. Galen was still influential.

Answering questions: Question 5 (b)

What you need to do

In the exam, you have to answer **either** Question 5 or Question 6. So, if you answered Question 5 (a) you **must** answer Question 5 (b).

Question 5 (b) will ask you to set out some **possible** answers to a question, weigh up the factors involved and make (and explain) your own **balanced judgement**. Examples of questions it might ask are:

- *How far were improvements in public health made by the Romans continued in the Middle Ages? Explain your answer.*
- *"Galen was still a strong influence on medicine during the Middle Ages." How far do you agree with this statement? Explain your answer.*

The question will be followed by an information box:

How far did the treatment of illness in the Middle Ages remain unchanged since Roman times? Explain your answer.

> You may use the following in your answer and any other information of your own:
> - St Bartholomew's Hospital in London was founded in 1123
> - by the 12th century there were training courses for doctors based on texts called the *Ars Medicinae*
> - medieval documents showed diagrams linking zodiac signs to different parts of the body.

This is the question we will use to practise our answers to Questions 5 (b).

How you do it
The best answers will look like this.

Let's try to write this kind of answer. Use the SuperFacts on the left. Start like this:

> In some ways, the treatment of illness in the Middle Ages was unchanged since Roman times. One thing that didn't change much was the cures people used for diseases.

> For example, people in the Middle Ages still believed in supernatural causes of illness, like diseases caused by God. So, sometimes, just like the Romans, they still used religious cures like prayers. Also, Galen's ideas were still influential in the Middle Ages. So people used purging or bloodletting to balance the humours. So, in these ways, treatment of illness was unchanged.

Now test yourself

Now finish off the answer to the question. We have put the titles of useful SuperFacts in the margin to help you. Look at pages 20–21 for the full versions of the SuperFacts.

> However, some things did change. For example, the training of … (i)

> This is an example of change because …(ii)

> Another thing that changed after Roman times was … (iii)

> This an example of change because … (iv)

Making the answer better

But you've not yet finished. There is no single 'right' answer to this question. However, the best answers always take an **overview** of the arguments and give their own, **balanced**, view. In this case, a good answer could finish:

> Overall, I think that medical treatment of illness didn't change that much. It is true that there were better doctors and more hospitals, but the most important thing was that the cures used were no different. The cures were the most important thing, but they didn't change much.

The final touch

Try writing your own final paragraph using the **opposite** view.

> Overall, I think that treatment of illness changed a lot between Roman times and the Middle Ages. I think this because … (v)

A well-written answer like this, which makes several points for and against, **supported by detail** and finishes with a sensible **balanced conclusion**, will reach the top level.

Results Plus
Top tip

Notice how we use **signposts** – introductory phrases that mirror the key phrases in the question – to make sure that the answer constantly focuses on the question. You should do the same. It helps you to keep focused and it shows the examiner that you have done so.

SuperFacts

Roman Britain did not have many doctors

The Roman army

Roman doctors did not have to be trained

In the early Middle Ages, doctors did not have to be trained

By the 12th century there were medical schools

There were over 1000 hospitals

Results Plus
Watch out!

Quality of written communication

When your answer to Question 5 (b) is marked, the quality of your written communication will always affect your mark.

To get to the top of each level of the mark scheme you have to:

* write effectively
* organise your thoughts coherently
* spell, punctuate and use grammar well.

The answer

You can find suggested answers to the tasks numbered (i), (ii), etc., on page 42.

Results**Plus**
Top tip

In the exam, students must answer **both** parts of either Question 5 or Question 6. If they answer one part from Question 5 and one part from Question 6, **only one part will be marked**.

Students who have studied the extension study *Medicine and public health from Roman Britain to c1350* should answer Questions 5 (a) and (b).

Students who have studied the extension study *Public Health c 1350 to present day* should answer Questions 6 (a) and (b).

SuperFacts

Cholera killed thousands in 1831 It was new to Britain and spread in dirty water. As industrial towns grew rapidly (Glasgow from 77,000 in 1801 to 329,000 in 1851; Leeds from 53,000 in 1802 to 172,000 in 1851), disease spread, especially in crowded slums with poor or no sanitation. The poor, weak from malnutrition, caught TB, typhoid and cholera easily.

The 1848 Public Health Act was passed after a bad outbreak of cholera earlier that year. It set up a General Board of Health to work until 1858. Towns could (but did not have to) set up a Board of Health, a town medical officer, sewers and rubbish removal.

The link between cholera and dirty water was proved by Dr John Snow in the 1854 cholera outbreak. He mapped deaths in Soho, London. Many of the dead had used the Broad Street water pump. Snow had the pump handle removed. The death rate dropped. He made links between different water companies and deaths, too.

Answering questions: Question 6 (a)

What you need to do
Remember, in the exam, you must answer **either** both parts of Question 5 or both parts of Question 6.

Question 6 (a) will ask you to **describe** or **explain** something. For example:

- *Why was cholera such a threat in the 19th century?*
- *Describe what progress was made in public health 1350–1750.*
- *How did government action improve public health in the 20th century?*

How you do it
Take the **first** question above as an example. The best answers to this question will:

- state **reasons** why cholera became such a threat in the 19th century.
- use **detailed information** to **explain how** they did this.

A good answer to this question might start like this.

> One reason cholera was such a threat was the rapid growth of industrial towns.

> Towns grew very quickly – Glasgow went from 77,000 in 1801 to 329,000 in 1851 – and they had crowded slums with poor or no sanitation. So cholera was more likely to happen and able to spread quickly when it did, killing more people.

The rest of the answer could be organised as below.

Use the SuperFacts on the left to write a sentence **explaining the reason** into each box. In the exam, you might write a longer explanation.

> Another reason cholera was a threat was the lack of government action.
>
> For example ... (i)

> They did not know how cholera spread until 1854.
>
> Only when ... (ii)

Listing a number of **reasons** why cholera became such a problem in the nineteenth century, and giving **details** to explain **how** these reasons made cholera more of a problem, will reach the top level.

Now test yourself

Practise a full examination answer. Write in each of the boxes to complete the answer.

Use the SuperFacts on the right to help you.

How did government action improve public health in the 20th century?

One way government action improved public health was the National Insurance Act.

This helped improve public health because... (iii)

Another way government action improved public health was the National Health Service.

This helped improve public health because... (iv)

Another way government action helped public health was ... (v)

(vi)

SuperFacts

Free healthcare for some of the unemployed came under the 1911 National Insurance Act. The government, workers and employers (in some industries) paid into a fund that paid the worker sick pay or unemployment benefit for a set period of weeks and gave free medicines. Medical care did not extent to the worker's family.

The National Health Service (NHS, 1948) was set up by Minister of Health Aneurin Bevan, despite resistance from doctors, who feared they would not be able to make a living. The NHS provided free healthcare for everyone, including dentistry and eye care, but had to charge for prescriptions, then eye care as costs rose.

Preventative measures since 1949 included more vaccines (polio, 1952; cervical cancer, 2008), government legislation to reduce pollution (the 1956 Clean Air Act) and health education (anti-smoking campaigns from the late 1960s on).

ResultsPlus
Top tip

Make sure that any other information you use is **relevant to the focus of the question**. So the focus of the question on this page is finding the links between **government actions** and improved health in the **twentieth century**. Actions by people not in government, or at other times than the twentieth century, will get no marks.

The answer
You can find suggested answers to the tasks numbered (i), (ii), etc., on page 43.

Answering questions: Question 6 (b)

What you need to do

In the exam, you have to answer either Question 5 **or** Question 6. So, if you answered Question 5 (a) you **must** answer Question 5 (b).

Question 6 (b) will ask you to set out some **possible answers** to a question, weigh up the factors involved and make (and explain) your own **balanced judgement**. Examples of questions it might ask are:

- *"There were no significant improvements in public health 1350–1750." How far do you agree with this statement? Explain your answer.*
- *How different was public health provision in the 19th and 20th centuries? Explain your answer.*

The question will be followed by an information box:

Why did attitudes to public health change during the middle of the nineteenth century? Explain your answer.

> You may use the following in your answer and any other information of your own:
> - the cholera epidemics of 1831 and 1848
> - Dr John Snow investigated an outbreak of cholera in 1854
> - The Great Stink of 1858.

This is the question we shall use to practise our answers to Question 6(b).

How you do it

The best answers will look like this.

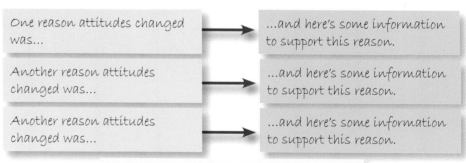

One reason attitudes changed was... → ...and here's some information to support this reason.

Another reason attitudes changed was... → ...and here's some information to support this reason.

Another reason attitudes changed was... → ...and here's some information to support this reason.

So, weighing up the different reasons for change, the most important one was ...

SuperFacts

Cholera killed thousands in 1831

Edwin Chadwick

Chadwick's report

Opponents to Chadwick's ideas

The 1848 Public Health Act

The titles of helpful SuperFacts on pages 22–23 are on the left. Start like this.

One reason attitudes towards public health changed in the mid-19th century was cholera.

The cholera outbreak of 1831 killed thousands. It prompted Edwin Chadwick to investigate the outbreak. He concluded that people needed clean water and the removal of sewage and rubbish to stay healthy. He said taxes should be spent on better housing, not workhouses. At first, he was supported by only a few newspapers and MPs. Some people, like taxpayers, opposed him. But, after another outbreak of cholera in 1848, the Public Health Act was passed. Cholera was therefore the trigger for a big change in attitudes towards public health.

Now test yourself

Now finish off the answer to the question. We have put the titles of useful SuperFacts in the margin to help you. Look at pages 22–23 for the full versions of the SuperFacts.

> *Another reason for the change in attitudes towards public health in the mid-19th century was the work of medical researchers like...* (i)

> *This medical research caused a change of attitudes because...* (ii)

> *Another reason attitudes to public health changed was...* (iii)

> *This changed attitudes towards public health because...* (iv)

Making the answer better

But you've not yet finished. There is no single 'right' answer to this question. However, the best answers will look at the interaction between the factors, and focus clearly on the question.

> *Overall, I think cholera was the key reason for changing people's attitudes towards public health. It started a chain of events. It was the reason Chadwick issued his famous report. This in turn led to the 1848 Public Health Act. This broke the principle of laissez faire and it set a precedent for the 1875 Public Health Act. So, in a way, it was cholera that started the change in attitude.*

The final touch

Try writing your own final paragraph using a **different** view.

> *Overall, I think the works of Snow and Pasteur were the main cause of changing attitudes towards public health. I think this because ...* (v)

A well-written answer like this, which makes several points for and against, **supported by detail** and finishes with a sensible **balanced conclusion** will reach the top level.

ResultsPlus
Top tip

Notice how we use **signposts** – introductory phrases that mirror the key phrases in the question – to make sure that the answer constantly focuses on the question. You should do the same. It helps you to keep focused and it shows the examiner that you have done so.

SuperFacts

The link between cholera and dirty water

Mounting evidence about dirt and disease

The 1875 Public Health Act

Louis Pasteur (see p13)

In the 'Great Stink' of 1858

Sewers were built rapidly after the Great Stink

ResultsPlus
Watch out!

Quality of written communication

When your answer to Question 6 (b) is marked, the quality of your written communication will always affect your mark.

To get to the top of each level of the mark scheme you have to:

- write effectively
- organise your thoughts coherently
- spell, punctuate and use grammar well.

The answer

You can find suggested answers to the tasks numbered (i), (ii), etc., on page 43.

Answers: Medicine and Treatment

Question 1

i) ... is that they used to think illness should be cured by religious treatments. This has changed. They now believe in scientific treatments for illness

ii) ... Source A, Gaddesden says he can cure toothache by writing religious words on the patient's jaw. I can infer from this that he thinks toothache can be cured by religious words. But Source B shows Pasteur working with a microscope and other scientific equipment. This shows that he must think there is a scientific cure for illness.

Question 2

i) ... because his germ theory (1861) showed what caused illness (germs). Also, in 1879, his team produced a chicken cholera vaccine.

ii) ... once people knew that germs caused disease and understood about vaccines fighting disease, they were able to look for new vaccines to treat diseases. Researchers found vaccines that could be used to treat typhoid (1896), TB (1906), diphtheria (1913) and measles (1964).

Questions 3 and 4

i) ... as more people did dissections, they found more and more information which contradicted the old ideas. So, Vesalius made detailed drawings of the inside of the human body. He showed that Galen's ideas were wrong about the structure of the heart, liver and lower jaw.

ii) ... they began to think about the body as a machine and made new discoveries about how the body worked. For example, William Harvey worked out how blood circulated by thinking about how mechanical pumps worked. Then he used the new thinking to do experiments that proved it.

iii) ... many more books could be produced, faster and more cheaply. Printed medical texts, such as Harvey's Anatomical Account of the Motion of the Heart and Vesalius' Fabric of the Human Body spread new knowledge. This encouraged more investigations and even more new knowledge.

Question 5 (a)

i) Something like:

... prayers or by making an offering to Salus, the god of health.

or

... going on a pilgrimage was something Christians believed could help a medical cure.

ii) Something like:

... it disapproved of dissection, which slowed down medical research.

or

... it approved of the work of Galen, which helped to spread medical ideas.

iii) The Romans believed in keeping clean. They saw a link between dirt and disease, though they did not know what the link was. So the Romans used public baths to stay clean and healthy. They had public baths (wealthy Romans had private baths). In the baths, they oiled themselves and scraped off the dirt with a strigil.

iv) The Romans saw a link between bad smells and disease, so they had clean public toilets. These had running water, with sewers or drains to take the dirty sewage away.

v) ... using clean, fresh water.

vi) The Romans thought bad, swampy water caused disease. So they had fresh water piped from a clean water supply. Towns had street fountains or wells where people could collect clean water.

Question 5 (b)

i) ... doctors was better.

ii) ...doctors weren't common in Roman Britain. The Roman army had doctors, but they did not treat civilians, so the head of the household did. Anyway, Roman doctors did not have to train. This had changed by the late Middle Ages. Medical schools taught the ideas of Galen and Muslim authors. By the 13th century, towns wanted proof of study from doctors.

iii) ... the provision of hospitals.

iv) ... only the Roman army had hospitals. In the Middle Ages, monks and nuns gave some medical care. By the end of the Middle Ages, there were 1,000 hospitals and 'houses' for special medical problems, like leprosy.

v) Something like:

... although they were still using some of the same treatments, like the herbal cures and blood-letting, by that time people were more likely to be treated by a trained doctor, who had studied anatomy, or in a proper hospital which specialised in their illness.

Question 6 (a)

i) Something like:

... even when the government did pass the 1848 Public Heath Act towns could, but did not have to, have a medical officer, proper sewers and rubbish removal.

ii) Something like:

... John Snow proved that the Broad Street pump was the source of an outbreak of cholera did people come to understand that they needed to get clean drinking water to avoid cholera.

iii) *... from 1911, the government, worker and employer paid into a fund that gave some workers sick pay and free medicine. This improved the health of workers because they could afford treatment and to stay off work while they were getting better.*

iv) *... it provided free healthcare for everyone, including (at first) dentistry and eye care. This meant even the poor could get treatment, so stayed healthier.*

v) *... by preventative measures.*

vi) *The government targeted certain health problems, like polio, cervical cancer and air pollution. It gave health education for problems like smoking.*

Question 6 (b)

i) *... Dr John Snow and Louis Pasteur.*

ii) *... they proved the link between cholera and dirty water. Snow showed the link between cholera deaths and dirty water at the Broad Street pump. Pasteur published his 1861 germ theory, linking germs and decay (and later, disease). This showed the need to reduce germs and clean up the water supply to improve public health.*

iii) *... the Great Stink of 1858.*

iv) *... in the summer of 1858, the Thames went down very low. The sun heated the sewage left behind (the river was full of it). It made the whole city smell. This caused the government to build new sewers. By 1865, it had 1,300 miles of sewers keeping the sewage away from people and improving their health.*

v) Something like:

... Chadwick's work never convinced the government to make permanent changes (the 1848 Public Health Act was only temporary). But, after 1850, John Snow's cholera research and Pasteur's germ theory (1861) caused the government to act. They made plans for sewers and water provision. The 1875 Public Health Act made these kinds of changes compulsory for all town councils.

Unit 3

The Unit 3 Exam:
The transformation of surgery c1845–c1918

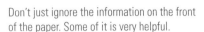
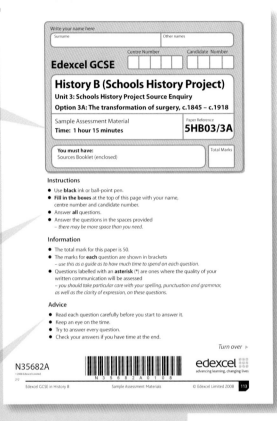

Write your name here

Surname

Other names

Edexcel GCSE

Centre Number   Candidate Number

History B (Schools History Project)
Unit 3: Schools History Project Source Enquiry
Option 3A: The transformation of surgery, c.1845 – c.1918

| Sample Assessment Material | Paper Reference |
| Time: 1 hour 15 minutes | **5HB03/3A** |

You must have:
Sources Booklet (enclosed)

Total Marks

Instructions

- Use **black** ink or ball-point pen.
- **Fill in the boxes** at the top of this page with your name, centre number and candidate number.
- Answer **all** questions.
- Answer the questions in the spaces provided
  – there may be more space than you need.

Information

- The total mark for this paper is 50.
- The marks for **each** question are shown in brackets
  – use this as a guide as to how much time to spend on each question.
- Questions labelled with an **asterisk** (*) are ones where the quality of your written communication will be assessed
  – you should take particular care with your spelling, punctuation and grammar, as well as the clarity of expression, on these questions.

Advice

- Read each question carefully before you start to answer it.
- Keep an eye on the time.
- Try to answer every question.
- Check your answers if you have time at the end.

Turn over ▶

N35682A

©2008 Edexcel Limited.
2/2

Edexcel GCSE in History B   Sample Assessment Materials   © Edexcel Limited 2008   113

Edexcel GCSE

History B (Schools History Project)
Unit 3: Schools History Project Source Enquiry
Option 3A: The transformation of surgery, c.1845 – c.1918

| Sample Assessment Material | Paper Reference |
| **Sources Booklet** | **5HB03/3A** |

Do not return this Sources Booklet with the question paper.

Turn over ▶

N35682A

©2008 Edexcel Limited.
2/2

Edexcel GCSE in History B   Sample Assessment Materials   © Edexcel Limited 2008   119

How the exam works

The exam for Unit 3 is quite different from the other exam papers in SHP History. This is because this paper tests your understanding of how historians use sources. There is less for you to learn before you go into the exam. Instead you have to use the sources you are given in the exam to answer the questions. So Unit 3 it is not about *how much you know, but what you know how to do.*

Sources are the raw material of history. Historians use them to work out what happened and why. But it isn't as simple as just looking at the sources, which may contradict themselves and one another, or even mislead. Historians need a range of skills to puzzle out the answers from lots of different sources. The Unit 3 exam tests that you have some of these skills.

There are five questions in the exam, and they will usually test the same skills in the same order (which is good news for you).

- **Question 1**, worth 6 marks, tests your ability to understand a source and to make an **inference** from it.

- **Question 2**, worth 8 marks, sees if you can understand the **portrayal** in a source – how the person who created it wanted it to influence people's opinion about the information given. The question may be put in different ways (e.g. 'How does the artist convey his view?' or 'How can you tell the author disapproves of [something]?') but it is always about understanding the message of the person who created the source and the reaction they wanted to produce.

- **Question 3**, worth 10 marks, asks you to **cross-refer** between sources.

- **Question 4**, worth 10 marks, asks you to judge the **utility** or **reliability** of sources.

- **Question 5** gives you a hypothesis about what happened, and asks you to judge **how far the sources support or prove it**.

Because the exam is different, this section of the revision book is different too. There are fewer SuperFacts. They have been chosen to give you a general context that should help you to deal with any set of sources you may be given.

Next, you have four pages to help you remember how to use sources. Finally, you practise answering questions.

ResultsPlus
Top tip

Context
To understand the context of a source is to see how it fits into the background of things that were happening when it was created.

For example, the cartoon on p.12 shows an imaginary scene – people growing cows or parts of cows from different parts of their body. Someone shown this cartoon who did not understand the context would be puzzled by it. Is this something like a modern-day horror film?

Using the caption and the context provided by your revision, you will know that when Jenner publicised his cow pox vaccination against smallpox, he faced a lot of opposition. You can understand this cartoon by putting it in its **context**: the opposition to Jenner's cowpox vaccine.

The Transformation of Surgery, c1845–c1918

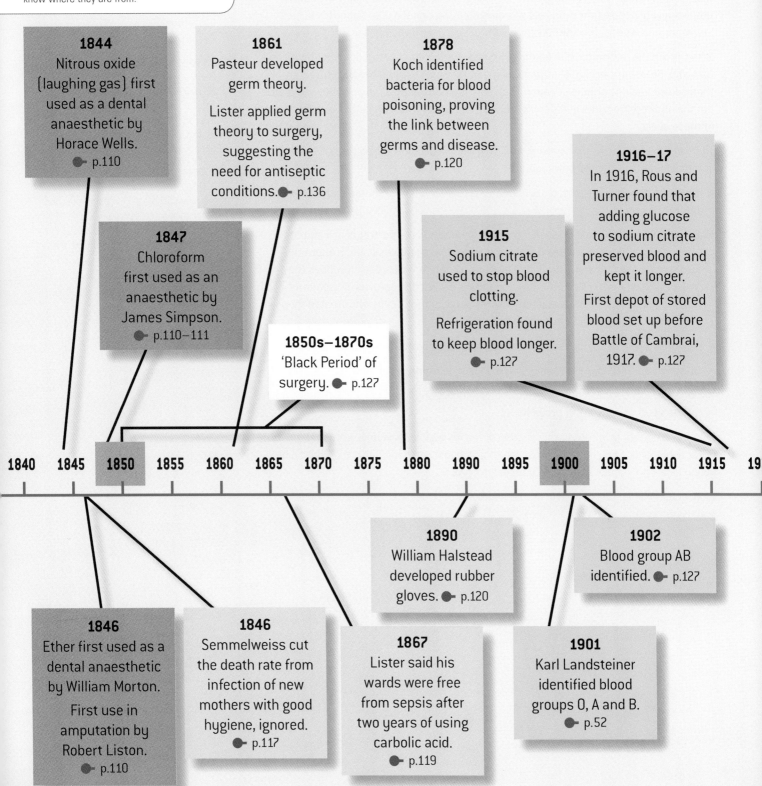

1844
Nitrous oxide (laughing gas) first used as a dental anaesthetic by Horace Wells.
p.110

1861
Pasteur developed germ theory.
Lister applied germ theory to surgery, suggesting the need for antiseptic conditions. p.136

1878
Koch identified bacteria for blood poisoning, proving the link between germs and disease.
p.120

1916–17
In 1916, Rous and Turner found that adding glucose to sodium citrate preserved blood and kept it longer.
First depot of stored blood set up before Battle of Cambrai, 1917. p.127

1847
Chloroform first used as an anaesthetic by James Simpson.
p.110–111

1915
Sodium citrate used to stop blood clotting.
Refrigeration found to keep blood longer.
p.127

1850s–1870s
'Black Period' of surgery. p.127

1840 1845 1850 1855 1860 1865 1870 1875 1880 1890 1895 1900 1905 1910 1915 19

1846
Ether first used as a dental anaesthetic by William Morton.
First use in amputation by Robert Liston.
p.110

1846
Semmelweiss cut the death rate from infection of new mothers with good hygiene, ignored.
p.117

1867
Lister said his wards were free from sepsis after two years of using carbolic acid.
p.119

1890
William Halstead developed rubber gloves. p.120

1901
Karl Landsteiner identified blood groups O, A and B.
p.52

1902
Blood group AB identified. p.127

Factors affecting developments in surgery

Factors that affected the development of surgery often depended on each other for the development to happen. For example, Lister's antiseptic carbolic spray relied on:

- scientific development (Pasteur's germ theory)
- technological work (the manufacture of a small, light spray)
- communication (Pasteur and Lister both had to spread their ideas among other doctors and researchers).

Below is a diagram to show how some surgical advances as a result of the First World War needed scientific development, technological work and communication to succeed.

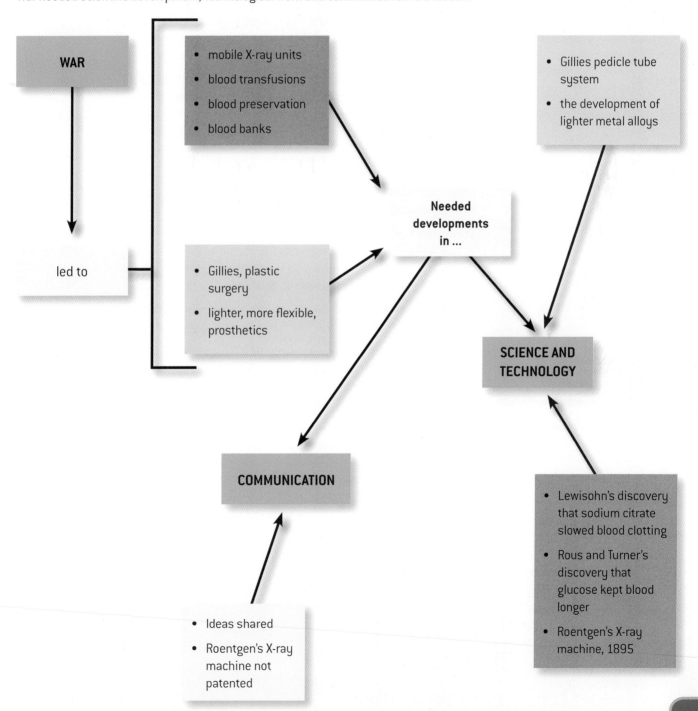

Section summary

Before the development of anaesthetics in the mid-19th century, there was little effective pain relief. Surgeons had to operate quickly to cut down the patient's pain, shock and blood loss. They did not go deep into the body, nor did they perform complicated procedures.

The first anaesthetic was nitrous oxide ('laughing gas'). It was followed by ether. Chloroform, first used in 1847, was an improvement and the most widely used.

edexcel ::: key terms

anaesthetic An anaesthetic is a drug given to a patient that stops them feeling pain during surgery.

general anaesthetic An anaesthetic that affects the whole body and makes the patient unconscious.

local anaesthetic An anaesthetic that affects only the part of the body being operated on.

opium This is a drug made from poppies which was given to patients to help dull pain before anaesthetics.

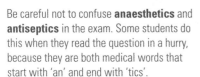

ResultsPlus
Watch out!

Be careful not to confuse **anaesthetics** and **antiseptics** in the exam. Some students do this when they read the question in a hurry, because they are both medical words that start with 'an' and end with 'tics'.

Need more help?

You can find a longer explanation of each SuperFact in your Edexcel textbook, *Schools History Project: Medicine and Surgery*. Look for this symbol ●–, which will give you the page number.

SuperFacts 1
Dealing with pain

SuperFacts are the key bits of information. Learn them and ask someone to test you.

There were no anaesthetics until the mid-19th century. Some doctors gave patients alcohol or opium, so they were less aware of the pain. The pain, and the shock and blood loss that came with it, meant doctors avoided operations. When they had to operate, other people held the patient down and doctors worked as fast as they could. ●– p.108

The most common surgery in the 19th century was amputation. Surgeons also cut out stones from the bladder, which is not very deep in the body. ●– p.108

The first suggested anaesthetic was nitrous oxide ('laughing gas'). Humphrey Davy discovered that it made you less aware of pain and suggested its use in surgery. It was first used as a dental anaesthetic by Horace Wells in 1844. ●– p.110

Ether was first used as an anaesthetic in September 1846. William Morton, a dentist in the USA, showed teeth could be painlessly extracted with it. He then successfully operated on a neck tumour. The first amputation to use ether as an anaesthetic was performed by Robert Liston in December 1846. ●– p.110

Ether had problems It sometimes made patients vomit and irritated the lungs, causing coughing even when unconscious. Patients often stayed unconscious for days. It was difficult to use because it was very flammable and needed to be transported in large, heavy glass bottles. ●– p.110

Chloroform was first used as an anaesthetic by James Simpson, a doctor in Edinburgh, in 1847. Queen Victoria popularised its use in childbirth when she used it in 1853 for the birth of her eighth child. However, it affected the heart and exact dosage was difficult. Some patients died of heart problems. ●– p.111

The chloroform inhaler, invented by Dr John Snow, controlled the dosage of chloroform, reducing the number of deaths from heart problems. ●– p.111

Some people did not welcome anaesthetics Some believed God wanted people to feel pain, especially in childbirth. The number of deaths after operations rose at first, as doctors needed experience to get the dosage right. Some people distrusted them because they were new and not all effects were known. ●– p.111

Cocaine was used as an anaesthetic in Europe from the 1850s, but was addictive. In 1884 it was found it could be used as a local anaesthetic, applied to the part of the body the surgeon wanted to numb. Novocaine, a version of cocaine that could be used as a local anaesthetic, was discovered in 1905. ●– p.111

SuperFacts 2
Dealing with infection

SuperFacts are the key bits of information. Learn them and ask someone to test you.

Infection was a huge problem in early 19th century operations. Surgeons wore old, bloodstained clothes. Everyone else wore ordinary clothes. The surgeon might wash his hands (or not), even his instruments, but nothing was germ-free. ●– p.117

The 'Black Period' of surgery (1850s–1870s) was when anaesthetics led to a rise in the number of operations because surgeons could use anaesthetics and so operate more easily. The death rate rose because doctors performed more complicated internal operations and there was a high infection rate. ●– p.117

Ignatz Semmelweiss, of Vienna General Hospital, noticed in 1846 that the death rate from infection after giving birth was much higher in the ward students worked on (often after dissecting corpses). He said the students were passing on infection. He made them wash their hands in a chlorinated solution before touching the women. The death rate dropped, but no one accepted his ideas; he even lost his job. ●– p.117

In 1861, Pasteur's germ theory linked germs and decay. Joseph Lister applied the idea to surgical infections, saying germ-ridden conditions caused infection. He said doctors should use antiseptic methods to fight germs. These methods used carbolic acid (which he had seen kill parasites in a sewage works) on bandages and in a spray. ●– p.118

Lister first used bandages soaked in carbolic acid in 1865, on the broken leg of an 11-year-old boy. He used bandages and the spray in his wards in Glasgow and, in 1867, said his wards were free of sepsis. In 1877, he moved to London and used his methods at King's College Hospital. ●– p.118

Lister's methods were quickly adopted in Germany and the USA, but many doctors in Britain opposed them. The strength of the solution was difficult to get right. The acid left skin cracked and sore. The equipment was expensive and, especially at first, heavy. Using the methods slowed down operations, so blood loss problems increased. ●– p.120

In 1878, Robert Koch identified the bacteria that caused blood poisoning, confirming the link between germs and disease. At the same time he developed the steam steriliser for surgical instruments (an aseptic advance). ●– p.120

The move to aseptic surgery was helped by the use of rubber gloves (1890, William Halstead), sterile gowns, face masks and head caps for doctors and nurses. Closed operating theatres and a sterile cloth over the patient also helped. ●– p.121

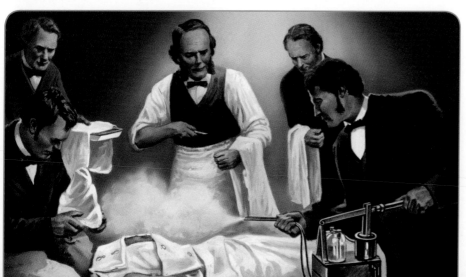

Section summary

Before the development of antiseptics, patients often died from infections. Soldiers at war more often died from operations than in battle. In 1861 Louis Pasteur's germ theory linked germs and decay. Joseph Lister applied the idea to surgical infections and announced that killing germs would reduce infection. Lister used carbolic acid as an antiseptic. Some doctors approved of his ideas and used them carefully, with good results. Others were not careful enough, or disliked the effects.

Once it was clear that germs were causing infections, doctors worked to provide **aseptic** (germ-free) operating conditions.

edexcel ▦ key terms

antiseptic A substance that fights germs that cause infection.

aseptic Free from germs.

sepsis The name given to infections (e.g. gangrene) caused by germs infecting an open wound.

Results Plus
Top tip

Be sure you know the difference between **'antiseptic'** and **'aseptic'**.

Antiseptics fight germs. Surgeons who used antiseptics were fighting the germs that they knew were in the air and getting into wounds during operations.

What surgeons really wanted was an aseptic operating theatre. Something is aseptic if it is germ-free. An aseptic environment would have no germs, so would not need antiseptics.

A modern artist's idea of Lister operating while using a carbolic spray.

edexcel :: key terms

blood transfusion Transferring blood into a patient from another person or animal.

cautery Using heat to seal a wound.

ligature A thread tied round a blood vessel to seal it.

tourniquet Something tied tightly around a limb to stop the blood flowing into it. This reduces blood loss in an amputation.

ResultsPlus
Top tip

When selecting SuperFacts to use in the exam, be careful to choose facts that are relevant to the exact focus of the question, **and** to be sure to link the SuperFact information to the sources. Remember, the Unit 3 exam expects you to use the sources first. These SuperFacts will help to put the sources you are given into context.

SuperFacts 3
Dealing with blood loss

SuperFacts are the key bits of information. Learn them and ask someone to test you.

Loss of blood was a common reason for death in the 19th century. Surgeons performing amputations tried to cut off the flow of blood to the limb beforehand with a clamp or tourniquet. Then they tried to stop blood loss by either sealing the blood vessels with heat (either hot oil or a hot iron) or tying them off with threads called ligatures. ● p.126

Blood transfusions replaced lost blood. Doctors had tried transfusions since the 17th century. Early transfusions were from animals to humans. They failed. Until blood types were discovered, human to human blood transfusions also had a low success rate. ● p.127

Blood types were first suggested by Karl Landsteiner in 1901. He suggested three types: A, B and O. A fourth type, AB, was added in 1902. ● p.127

Blood typing was little help to surgery at first. Surgeons who wanted to perform a blood transfusion had to test for the patient's blood type and then find someone willing to give blood who was of the same blood type – fast. Often this just wasn't possible in time. Doctors needed to find a way to stop blood clotting so they could store it. ● p.127

During the First World War (1914–18) a doctor from the USA, Richard Lewisohn, who had been using sodium citrate to thin blood during transfusions, suggested using it to store blood to set up blood banks for war surgeons. The blood had to be used quite quickly, but the stored blood still saved thousands of lives. ● p.127

Sodium citrate-treated blood was found to keep longer when it was refrigerated. In 1916, Rous and Turner found that adding glucose to the blood meant it lasted longer, so the army could call on the public to make blood donations when they were planning an attack. ● p.127

The first blood depot was set up in 1917, just before the Battle of Cambrai. It used type O blood, which had been proved to be safe to transfuse to all blood types. ● p.127

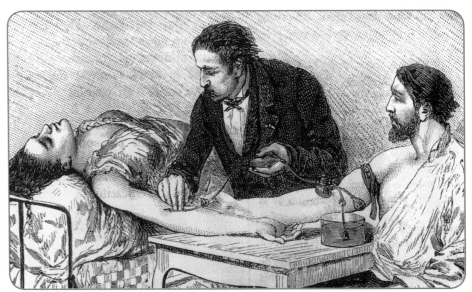

A drawing of an actual blood transfusion made in 1882. The patient had been slowly losing blood since giving birth to twins over a month before. Blood types had not been discovered, but the donor was of the same type, by chance. The patient survived.

SuperFacts 4 Factors influencing these developments

SuperFacts are the key bits of information. Learn them and ask someone to test you.

War puts pressure on surgeons They have to work in makeshift conditions and deal with many more patients. However, they do get a lot more experience of a wide range of injuries. Not only do they improve their techniques, they often have to invent new techniques – some of which turn out to be better than the old ones. ●– p.132

Antiseptic solutions In the First World War many wounds were deep wounds, caused by explosives, often with cloth or metal trapped in them. Operating conditions were not germ-free. So wounds often became infected. Doctors did not have carbolic acid; they found washing the wounds with a salt solution was the best antiseptic. ●– p.133

Harold Gillies (a doctor from New Zealand) used plastic surgery techniques developed in France to do facial reconstructions. He kept careful records, photos and drawings of his methods. His pedicle tube system allowed him to grow skin grafts. ●– p.133

Prosthetic limbs were improved during the First World War (over 41,000 men in the British armed forces lost a limb). Limbs were made from light metal alloys and new mechanisms were developed to make movement easier. ●– p.133

Scientific discoveries were important to progress in surgery (e.g. Pasteur's germ theory set off Lister's work on antiseptics, which reduced the death rate). Anaesthetics and the ability to store blood for transfusions came from scientific research. ●– p.134

Technological discoveries have helped surgery (e.g. more precise measurement of drug doses and X-raying). ●– p.134

The use of X-rays (discovered by Wilhelm Roentgen in 1895) spread rapidly because he did not take out a patent on his discovery. They showed war surgeons where bullets and shrapnel were in the body, so mobile X-ray units were developed during the First World War. ●– p.134

Hypodermic needles (invented by Alexander Wood in 1853) allowed doctors to give carefully measured doses of a drug. They could also use the needle to take blood samples from the body for testing. ●– p.135

Communicating ideas was vital for the progress of medicine. This was done by medical journals (e.g. *The Lancet*), newspaper articles (e.g. Queen Victoria's use of chloroform) and medical conferences. It was also important for people to keep careful records of their work and be willing to share their ideas. ●– p.136–137

Section summary

There are certain factors that have affected the progress of medicine and surgery all through time. Among these are war, communications and science and technology.

edexcel ::: key terms

patent When inventors register their invention with the patent office ('take out a patent'), the patent office stops other people copying their invention for profit.

pedicle tube An early skin graft technique. A flap of skin is cut from a 'donor area' near the area that needs new skin. One end is left in place. The other end is connected to the area that needs new skin. The flap is sewn into a tube to keep the skin alive. The skin keeps on growing. When it has grown enough, it is cut away from the donor area, opened out and stitched into place.

ResultsPlus
Watch out!

When considering the role of factors in medical development, be careful to consider the way the factors help and hinder progress. You should also remember that there is very seldom only one factor affecting progress. There are usually links between factors. For example, scientific advances allowed for blood storage, but it was not until the First World War that countries invested in developing this for large-scale use.

Need more help?

You can find a longer explanation of each SuperFact in your Edexcel textbook, *Schools History Project: Medicine and Surgery*. Look for this symbol ●–, which will give you the page number.

Using sources in the Unit 3 exam

When you take the exam you will have two booklets, a question booklet for writing your answers in and a sources booklet. **Do not** start by reading Question 1, looking at Source A and then answering the question. **Instead, the best way to start is to spend a few minutes studying ALL the sources**.

The first thing you will find is not a source at all, it is the **Background information**.

Background information

When anaesthetics began to be used in the nineteenth century, they led to huge changes in the way operations were carried out. Many people thought that this was an important advance in surgery but some people opposed the idea of anaesthetics.

The sources in this paper give you a range of views about these developments and provide the opportunity for you to decide for yourself whether the use of anaesthetics was an important breakthrough in surgery.

This is how the Background information is presented in the paper.

Don't skip the background information. It is there for a purpose: **the examiner is telling you what the paper is about.** In this case, the paper is about the importance of anaesthetics in the development of surgery. But the background does more than that. It also tells you that:

- anaesthetics led to changes in the way operations were carried out
- many people thought that anaesthetics were an important advance in surgery which would lead to progress
- however, others were opposed to the use of anaesthetics.

The background information is important in one other way. **It is the only thing in the sources booklet you can trust completely**. You need to be prepared to consider how accurate a picture the sources give.

This brings us to the most important part of the paper – the sources.

Watch out!

The source heading and caption for the next source are often directly underneath a source. Be careful not to mix them up and look at the wrong source. The caption comes before a source for a reason. **Read the caption first, then the source**. It will make more sense when you know more about who made the source and when.

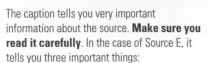

Top tip

The caption tells you very important information about the source. **Make sure you read it carefully**. In the case of Source E, it tells you three important things:

- **who** wrote the source – Queen Victoria
- **when** she wrote it – 1853
- **where** she wrote it – in her journal
- **some context** – it was the birth of her eighth child.

Source E: From Queen Victoria's journal, 1853, describing her reaction when she was given chloroform for the birth of her eighth child.

> 'Dr Snow gave me the blessed chloroform and the effect was mild, calming and beautiful beyond belief.'

Source F: From *For Fear of Pain : British Surgery 1790 – 1850* by Peter Stanley, 2003.

> It is possible that surgeons only used chloroform in the 1850s because patients demanded it. James Simpson collected statistics from several hospitals and was able to show that anaesthesia made the most serious operations half as dangerous. It kept patients from pain and also saved many of them from death.

This is how sources are presented in the paper.

Key skills for using sources

Inference

To make an inference is to work something out from a source that the source doesn't actually tell you or show you.

For example: The picture on page 49 **shows** you an operation with a carbolic spray being used. You can infer that the surgeon believed in the germ theory of disease from the use of carbolic spray, which was used to kill microbes and stop infection.

Now you try with Source B on page 71.

> (i) Give an example of something Source B shows you. Explain how it shows you.

> (ii) Give an example of something you can infer from Source B, and explain why.

Portrayal

Working out how a source was originally created to give a particular impression or message is called **portrayal**. It builds on inference of the type used in Question (i), but this time the focus is on **how** the author, artist or photographer has put the source together to give a particular impression.

For example: The **message** of the picture on page 49 is that Lister was a hero and a careful surgeon. The way the artist **portrays** this is by putting Lister in the middle of the picture, highlighted by the light and looking calm and in control. It also focuses on the carbolic spray in the right and centre foreground.

> (iii) What is the message of Source B?

> (iv) How has the photographer portrayed this message?

Need more help?

Using the sources with this exercise
From now on, you will be using the sources for *The Transformation of Surgery* on pages 69, 71 and 73 of this book. They have been printed like this so you can cut them out to keep in front of you while you work on the sources, without having to keep turning back and forth in the book. Be careful, though: **don't lose the pages**, because you will need them for all the work on Unit 3.

Results Plus
Watch out!

Using the sources in the paper
Questions 1 to 4 all use specific sources. Question 5 asks you to use particular sources and 'any other sources you find helpful'. **Be careful to use the sources referred to in the question.** You won't get any credit for writing about Source E in a question that asks you about Sources A, B and C only.

When you refer to a source, make it clear which one you mean. Say 'in Source A', or 'Source D says…'. If you want to quote from a source to prove your point, put the bit of the source you are quoting in quotation marks.

So **don't** say: A hospital went from 80% of wounds being infected to no wounds being infected…**Do** say: In Source C, a hospital in Munich went from 80% of wounds being infected to no wounds being infected…

The answer
You can find suggested answers to the tasks numbered (i), (ii), etc., on page 67.

Cross-referencing

Cross-referencing is the skill of comparing what two or more sources say about the same thing, or whether one or more supports another source. You will need to use this skill in all the questions which use two or more sources.

How you do it

When you cross-refer you need to look for things that agree, or things that don't agree, between the sources. For example:

> **Does Source F support the impression given in Source E that Lister's antiseptic spray was impractical?**

Source F **does support** Source E:

- ... because Source F says that it had 'disadvantages that even Lister acknowledged' and that when used with chloroform it gave off chlorine gas. This sounds very impractical.

But it **doesn't support** it completely:

- ... because Source F says that Lister's spray was used all over the world which wouldn't have happened if it was totally impractical.

Now you try, with a different question and different sources.

> **How far does Source B support Source G's view that antiseptic and aseptic methods were used by all surgeons?**

Ways they do agree: (v)

Ways they do not agree: (vi)

Cross-referencing won't give you the full answer to the question, you need to think about the **utility** and **reliability** of the sources as well.

Utility (usefulness, value)

This is quite straightforward. The only thing to remember is that **utility depends on the question**. So, starting with the question you want to answer, you just need to decide whether the source tells you anything useful or not.

For example (using the sources on pages 69, 71 and 73):

How did the techniques for doing surgery change from about 1860–1880?

- Source A – useful
- Source B – not useful
- Source C – useful
- Source D – useful

- Source E – useful
- Source F – useful
- Source G – not useful

Now you try, in the box below.

How common was the use of Lister's carbolic spray?
Are the sources useful to help you consider this question?

(vii)

Reliability

Testing a source for reliability is about thinking whether you can believe the source or not. What are the clues to look for?

- **Provenance** – who created the source and why?
- **Language** is a useful clue – often bias in a source shows up in its choice of language.
- **Selection** is a very powerful clue – sources don't tell us everything, and the person who created the source probably chose what to include and what to leave out. This can be just as true of a photograph as of a written source. A photographer decides which bit of what is happening to photograph and a newspaper editor decides which photograph to use. For example, in a demonstration, they could choose to show thousands of people protesting peacefully or a few people starting a fight with the police. The two photographs would give very different impressions of what happened.

Reliability affects what a source is useful for. An unreliable source might not be useful for facts – but it tells you useful things about the opinions of the person who created it.

Repeat the exercise you did for utility. This time consider reliability as well as utility.

Were Lister's ideas immediately accepted by all surgeons?
Are the sources useful and reliable?

(viii)

To make it easier to think about, we have just looked at cross-referencing, utility, and reliability separately. Very often, in the exam, you need to combine them all – how useful is a source that isn't reliable?

The answer
You can find suggested answers to the tasks numbered (i), (ii), etc., on page 67.

An **inference** is a judgement made from the source, which is not directly stated by it.

A **supported** inference is one that uses detail from the source to prove the inference.

Consider this example:

Source A: 'Tom was very rude to his friend's mother. The mother was angry and said she was going to tell Tom's mother what had happened.'

Question: *What does Source A tell us about Tom?*

Information: *Source A tells us Tom was very rude to his friend's mother.* [This is directly stated in the source, so it's not an inference.]

An inference could be: *Source A tells me that Tom is in serious trouble and is likely to be punished.* [The source does not directly tell us this, but we can infer that it is likely].

A supported inference could be: *Source A tells me Tom is in serious trouble and likely to be punished. I can infer this because his friend's mother was going to tell his mother he'd been very rude. His Mum wouldn't like him behaving like that, so she would be cross and punish him.* [An inference, with supporting details quoted from the source.]

Answering questions: Question 1

What you need to do

Question 1 will always ask: **What can you learn from Source A about [something]?**

The best answers:

- not only extract **information** from the source
- but also make **inferences** from the source [*see Top tip box*]
- and **support** those inferences with detail from the source.

Note: make sure you answer the question. You can't just make any inference from the source; it has to be about the subject of the question.

How you do it

Let's practise.

>*Study Source A. What can you learn from Source A about surgery in the 1870s?*

Source A: A painting of an operation in an American hospital in 1875.

A possible answer

Here is a possible answer to the question on the opposite page.

Inference	Supporting detail
I can learn from Source A that surgery in the 1870s was a team activity.	I can infer this because Source A shows one man using a saw, two with scalpels, another, possibly the anaesthetist, at the patient's head and two others around the patient. It seems they used a team of people to do surgery.

Notice how the answer:

- says what we can infer from the source
- gives supporting detail to explain why we can make this inference.

Now test yourself

Let's practise making supported inferences.

Here's another inference which could be made from Source A.

Write the **supporting detail (i)** for the inference.

I can learn from Source A that there were many sources of infection during surgery in the 1870s.	(i)

This time, we have provided the supporting detail.

Write the **inference (ii)** you can make from the supporting detail.

(ii)	I can infer this because the surgeons are men, all the other people around the bed are men and all the onlookers taking notes are men.

In the exam, one inference with support scores well.

You will usually need two supported inferences for top marks.

Results Plus
Top tip

Notice how, in our answers, we use key phrases such as *'I can infer from Source A that…'* and *'I can infer this because…'*. These **signposts** show how you are answering the question and make your answer easier to follow. Use them in your answers to help the examiner.

The sources

From now on, you will be using the sources on pages 69, 71 and 73 of this book. Cut them out so you can have them in front of you while you work on the sources. **Be careful not to lose the pages**, because you will need them for all the work on Unit 3.

The answer

You can find suggested answers to the tasks numbered (i), (ii), etc., on page 67.

Answering questions: Question 2

What you need to do

Question 2 will ask you to explain why a source was created and what its message was.

It could ask about the message given by a source or the purpose of a source.

Let's look at an example.

Study Source B.

> *How has the photographer shown that this is aseptic surgery? Explain your answer using Source B.*

Source B: A photograph of a hospital operating theatre.

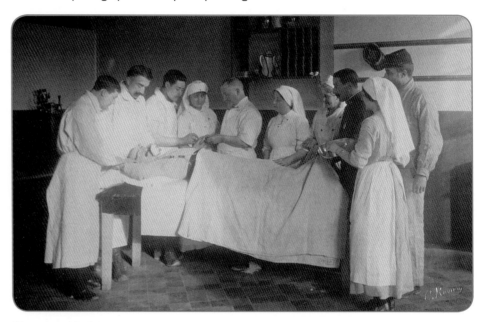

How you do it

Study the source carefully and look for the way the photographer has tried to put his or her message over.

Now test yourself

Let's use the question above to practise.

Step 1 is to remind yourself what the subject of the question is. In this case, it is what tells us that this is aseptic surgery.

First work out what the details are that tell us. Make a list of them.

(i)

ResultsPlus
Watch out!

Don't confuse 'message' and 'purpose'.

The **message** of a source is:

- the impression it gives
or
- what it is trying to say.

The **purpose** of a source is what the person who created it was trying to achieve – the effect that person wanted the source to have.

If you understand the **message** of a source, this gives you a clue to its **purpose**.

It is useful to write this list down before writing your answer.

Once you have written the list, **Step 2** is to explain what you have seen to the examiner. Look at your list. Are things in the best order? Is there anything else you could have noticed. After a moment's further thought, write your answer.

In your first sentence, tell the examiner what you are writing about **(ii)**.

Then go on to not just list, but **explain**, your reasons **(iii)**.

(ii)

(iii)

The answer
You can find suggested answers to the tasks numbered (i), (ii), etc., on page 67.

An answer like this, which **explains** the **ways** the source achieves its purpose, will get top marks.

Read the question carefully to be sure what you should cross-reference between.

- Some questions ask **how far one source supports another** about a particular view. In that case, you must cross-refer between the sources.

- Some questions ask **how far several sources support** a statement. In that case, you have to cross-refer between the sources and the statement and each other.

Cross-reference
Cross-referring between two or more sources means checking what different sources say about the same thing.

So, if one source says Lister's methods caused a drop in the death rate, then we can cross-reference this in the other sources. This means we can look to see if they say the same thing – or something different.

- If you cross-refer among lots of sources and they all agree about something, this encourages you to believe it.

- If you cross-refer among lots of sources and they disagree, then you may have to be more careful about the conclusions you make from them.

Answering questions: Question 3

What you need to do
Question 3 will ask you to **compare** two or more sources to answer a question.

For example:

> *How far does Source C agree with Source D [about something]?*

or

> *How far do Sources A, C and F agree [about something]?*

The best answers will:

- first, **cross-refer** between the sources – compare what they say to find ways in which the sources **do** and **do not** support each other; and
- second, consider **how reliable** the sources are.

How you do it
Use Sources C and D (cut out from pages 69, 71 and 73 of this book). Consider the following question:

> *How far do Sources C and D suggest that Lister's methods produced a dramatic and rapid reduction in the death rate?*

First, let's **cross-refer** between the sources.

We have done this below, showing ways in which the sources **support** the idea that Lister's methods produced a dramatic and rapid reduction in the death rate.

> The hospital in Source C had a 'horrifying' death rate 'at first', with high levels (80%) of wounds getting gangrene and pyaemia. Then, within a week after using Lister's methods, the gangrene stopped altogether, showing a rapid reduction in infection and implying a dramatic drop in the death rate. Source D supports the idea of a dramatic reduction in the death rate, from 45% to 15%. That is dramatic. And it says it was due to Lister's methods, just like Source C.

Now you try. Write a paragraph saying how the sources **do not support** the view that Lister's methods produced a dramatic and rapid reduction in the death rate.

> But the sources do not completely support the view that Lister's methods produced a rapid and dramatic reduction in the death rate. For example, ...
> (i)

An answer like those we've produced so far, which cross-refers between sources showing both support **and** lack of support, will get a good mark. However, the best answers go one step further.

The final step

So far, our answer says **how much** support the sources give to the suggestion of a rapid and dramatic reduction in the death rate. But they can only really support the view in question if they are **reliable**.

Read about **reliability** in the *Top tip box* on this page.

Now consider the **provenance** and **content** of Source C and Source D.

We've written our conclusions about the reliability of **Source C** for this question.

> Source C is probably reliable, but the language used suggests that there might be exaggeration. For example, it says that the death rate 'was horrifying' and 'Not another case of gangrene appeared'. You suspect that the doctor was a supporter of Lister's ideas. But the quotes are in an academic study of surgery in a textbook, so you would expect the author to have checked that what the source says is reliable.

Now you consider **Source D**. Write your conclusions about how reliable it is for this question.

> There are reasons for thinking that Source D could be reliable or that it could be unreliable. For example... [ii]

The best answer will finish with an **overall judgement**.

This should be a very short summary of whether the sources do or do not support a rapid and dramatic drop in the death rate and whether you believe them.

Write your own conclusion in the box below.

> In conclusion, I think... [iii]

An answer like this, which considers the level of support in the sources (and how reliable they are) and then gives an overall judgement, will reach the top level.

ResultsPlus
Top tip

Reliability
The reliability of a source is how far you can trust what it says about the thing you are studying.
You can test the reliability of a source by looking at its **provenance** and **content**.

Provenance means:
- who wrote/produced it
- where and when
- what kind of source it is
- why it was produced (its *purpose*)

Content includes:
- the language it uses
- signs of exaggeration
- *selection* – things it includes or leaves out
- how **typical** it is.

Asking these questions about a source will give you ideas about how reliable it is.

Typicality
Typicality is one aspect of the content of a source that affects how much you rely on it. If the information in one source is much the same as the information in other similar sources, then your source is typical. This would encourage you to rely on it more. If information selected for inclusion in a source is very different from information in other similar sources, then your source is not typical. This might lead you to be more careful about the conclusions you make from it.

The answer
You can find suggested answers to the tasks numbered (i), (ii), etc., on page 67.

To reach a judgement about which of two sources is most useful for a particular enquiry, you need to consider two things:

- the content of the source
- the reliability/typicality of the source.

Considering the content of the sources is only the first step. A source can give a lot of relevant information, but this information is not useful for the enquiry if the source was lying, or the only one of its kind.

Notice how we use key phrases such as '*is useful because*' and '*seems reliable because*' in our answers. These **signposts** show how you are answering the question and make your answer easier to follow. Use them in your answers to help the examiner.

Answering questions: Question 4

Question 4 will usually ask which of two sources is more useful to a historian studying a certain subject.

What you need to do

You need to consider both of the sources.

- Firstly, consider how much useful information they contain for the particular enquiry in the question.
- Secondly, consider how **reliable** that information is; how much do you trust it?

How you do it

Use Sources E and F (cut out from pages 69, 71 and 73 of this book). Consider the following question:

> *How useful are Sources E and F to a historian studying the problems of using carbolic spray? Explain your answer, using Sources E and F.*

Read the *Top tip box* about utility on this page.

Now write two paragraphs to say how much useful and relevant information there is/is not in Sources E and F (remember to give examples from the sources).

Sources E and F are both useful because... (i)

However, there is a limit to how useful Sources E and F are. For example... (ii)

Check your answer against the sample answer on page 67 before you continue.

So far, our answer has considered the content of Sources E and F. But this information is only useful if we can trust it.

So Step 2 of our answer involves considering whether the useful information is reliable.

Assessing the **provenance** and **content** of the sources will help you decide how much to trust them.

Think about the **provenance** of Sources E and F. Write a paragraph saying if this makes you trust the information in these sources about the problems of carbolic spray. Remember, you need to think about who wrote each source, when and where they wrote them and what kind of sources they are. You also need to consider why the sources were written.

> The information in Sources E and F is only useful if we can trust it. In this case... (iii)

Now look at the **content** of Sources E and F. Write a paragraph saying whether this makes you trust the information in the sources about problems with the carbolic spray.

Remember, you need to think about the language of the sources, what they might choose to put in or leave out, and how typical you think they are.

> The content... (iv)

Answers that assess how useful the sources are by considering the information the sources give (and do not give), and also consider the reliability of the information, will reach the top level.

Results Plus
Top tip

Reliability
Refer to the *Top tip box* on page 61 for help about reliability.

Results Plus
Watch out!

Sometimes Question 4 will ask you only about **reliability**. For example, the question in this spread could have been:

How reliable are Sources E and F as evidence of the problems using carbolic spray? Explain your answer using Sources E and F.

In this case, you do not need to consider utility to answer the question. Just do parts **(iii)** and **(iv)** of our sample answer.

The answer
You can find suggested answers to the tasks numbered (i), (ii), etc., on page 67.

Quality of written communication

When your answer to Question 5 is marked, the quality of your written communication will always affect your mark.

To get to the top of each level of the mark scheme you have to:

- write effectively
- organise your thoughts coherently
- spell, punctuate and use grammar well.

Answering questions: Question 5

What you need to do

Question 5 will always:

- give you a **statement** or ask a **question**
- and then ask you to make a **judgement** about the statement or question
- by referring to **the sources** and **your own knowledge**.

How you do it

You must use **the sources <u>and</u> your own knowledge** in your answer.

The best answers to this kind of question will always look like this.

> They will make a **balanced judgement** about the statement. They will...

> show some ways the sources support one side of the argument, then…

> The answers will then show some ways in which the sources support the other side of the argument.

> give **evidence** for this from the sources and your own knowledge, then…

> They will give **evidence** for this from the sources and your own knowledge, then…

> say how **strong** the evidence is e.g. by discussing how **reliable** or **unreliable** it is.

> say how **strong** the evidence is e.g. by discussing how **reliable** or **unreliable** it is.

> Finally, the answer will weigh the evidence for and against the statement and **give an overall, balanced judgement**.

Test yourself

Use the sources cut out from pages 69–73. Consider the following question:

> **'The antiseptic system developed by Joseph Lister was widely used and made surgery safer.'**
> **How far do you agree with this statement?**
> **Use your own knowledge, Sources C, F and G and any other sources you find helpful.**

On the following page, we have provided an answer to this question. Your task is to:

a) cut out the paragraphs provided and sort them into the correct order

b) fill in the missing parts of the paragraphs, to show that you understand how the answer should be constructed.

Paragraph 1

For example, (i) _____ says that antiseptic methods ended hospital gangrene at von Nussbaum's hospital in Munich. Source G says that, by 1900, antiseptic methods were used by all surgeons and Source F says (ii) _____
_____

Paragraph 2

The sources show that Lister's methods made surgery safer by making people aware of the need to fight germs. Many people used his antiseptic ideas and developed their own ideas (like rubber gloves).

Paragraph 3

However, some parts of the sources suggest that the impact of Lister's methods was limited. The main thing that limited their influence was that (iii) _____
_____

Paragraph 4

Having considered the sources and my own knowledge, I think they agree that Lister's methods did increase safety. But problems like the unpleasant vapours, the expense and the extra work meant the methods were not used as widely as they might have been.

Paragraph 5

I trust the sources for the reasons I have already given.

Paragraph 6

For example, Source F says that surgeons didn't like working with the spray because (iv) _____
_____

Paragraph 7

The sources use different types of evidence (Source C quotes doctors from the time) and yet they agree, broadly, which seem to make them reliable. They agree it made things safer, but was difficult to use, especially the spray. Source E supports F on this, saying (v) _____
_____ and possibly by comparing Sources A and B, which show (vi) _____
_____ _____. From my own knowledge I know that another problem was (vii) _____
_____

ResultsPlus
Top tip

Remember that, in Question 5, the examiner wants you to present a balanced argument. When you are asked if you agree that the sources support a statement, you need to:

- find evidence that they support the statement **and** find evidence they don't support the statement

- consider the reliability of the sources you are using

- always finish the answer with a conclusion which explains your judgement, based on your analysis of the content and reliability of the sources.

The answer
You can find suggested answers to the tasks numbered (i), (ii), etc., on page 67.

Answers: The transformation of surgery c1845–c1918

Key skills for using sources

i) All the people are wearing clean white clothes and the whole room looks clean.

ii) Surgeons who operated like this, in clean conditions, with special clothes, were following Lister's ideas and doing antiseptic surgery, even trying to be aseptic.

iii) That this was an operation done under antiseptic (even trying to be aseptic) conditions.

iv) Source G says they stopped operating 'in blood-caked clothes in dingy rooms with sawdust covered floors'. Source B shows this: clean room, floor and clothes. Source G talks about 'face-masks, rubber gloves and surgical gowns' and in B they are wearing gowns and the surgeon might be putting on gloves.

v) Source G says they wore face masks, which no-one is B is doing, and it said 'all surgeons' did this and this surgeon isn't.

vi) Source G says they wore face masks, but nobody in Source B is wearing one. More importantly, Source G says these things were done by all surgeons, but here we only see one surgeon, and he isn't wearing a face mask.

vii) A – not useful; B – useful; C – useful; D – useful; E – useful; F – useful; G – not useful.

viii) A – useful if reliable; B – useful if reliable; C – useful and reliable; D – useful and reliable; E – useful and reliable; F – useful and reliable; G – not useful.

Question 1

i) I can infer this because the surgeons have their normal clothes on and are not wearing special gloves or masks.

ii) I can infer from Source A that surgery was an activity which was dominated by men in the 1870s.

Question 2

i) All are wearing clean surgical gowns; the women wear caps over their hair; the surgeon is putting on rubber gloves; the room and floor are clean and uncluttered.

ii) The photographer shows this is aseptic surgery in a number of ways.

iii) All are wearing clean surgical gowns rather than ordinary clothes that could bring in disease.
The women wear caps over their hair to stop any infection transferring to the wound.
The surgeon is putting on rubber gloves so there can be no infection transferred by his hands.
The room and floor are clean and uncluttered so they can be sterilised.

Question 3

i) ... it shows a reduction in deaths years later. So Source D does not really prove a <u>rapid</u> reduction, while Source C is talking about a rapid reduction in infection. We can infer a drop in the death rate, but we can't know if all those not infected actually survived.

ii) ... the figures in Source D are Lister's own figures. He could have shown more people surviving than really did, to promote his own methods. But Lister hasn't shown them all surviving. And he must have known that other people at the hospital would say if he lied. Finally, from my own knowledge, other sources suggest his methods affected the death rate like this. So, overall, I trust Source D, I think it is reliable.

iii) ... generally, Sources C and D agree that Lister's methods reduced the death rate, although I don't think they completely support the idea that this drop was 'dramatic' and 'rapid'. They both seem reliable enough.

Question 4

i) ... they tell us about the problems of using carbolic spray. In Source E, it says how the spray was so 'repellent' that some surgeons didn't want to use it and how it caused 'heated debates'. Source F tells us how it created chlorine gas (which burned the eyes, nose and throat) when used with chloroform.

ii) ... they tell us what the problems were, but they don't tell us how widely the spray was used or what doctors did to overcome the problems.

iii) ... both seem to have reliable provenance. Source E is a published book and the facts should have been checked. Source F comes from the Australasian College of Surgeons official website.

iv) ... focuses on the problems and uses words like 'repellent'. Source F uses more moderate language and seems more balanced (so probably is more reliable). While it tells us the problems it also says the spray was 'used all over the world'.

Question 5

The correct order for the paragraphs is: 2, 1, 7, 3, 6, 5, 4
The missing words are:

i) Source C

ii) Lister's steam spray came to be used all over the world.

iii) the spray was unpleasant to work with ('repellent' Source E), especially when it was used at the same time as chloroform as an anaesthetic (Source F).

iv) it gave off an unpleasant vapour at the best of times, and when used with chloroform the vapor made a gas that made the throat burn when breathed in.

v) surgeons found the spray 'repellent'

vi) ... people were taking more precautions against germs in Source B (clean uniforms and room, no audience).

vii) any example from your own knowledge; e.g. it burned the hands (Halstead invented rubber gloves to protect the hands of his fiancée, a nurse).

Background information

One of the biggest problems a surgeon faces is sepsis: infection during an operation or just after it. In 1861, an English doctor, Joseph Lister, applied Pasteur's germ theory to surgery, showing that killing germs during operations reduced the death rate of patients. He developed an antiseptic system, including a spray that covered everything with carbolic acid. He treated the wound with carbolic-soaked dressings. Surgeons were divided as to whether this was the answer to preventing sepsis.

The sources in this paper present a range of views to give you the opportunity to decide if the use of antiseptics made surgery safer.

Source A: A painting of an operation in an American hospital in 1875.

Source B: A photograph of a hospital operating theatre.

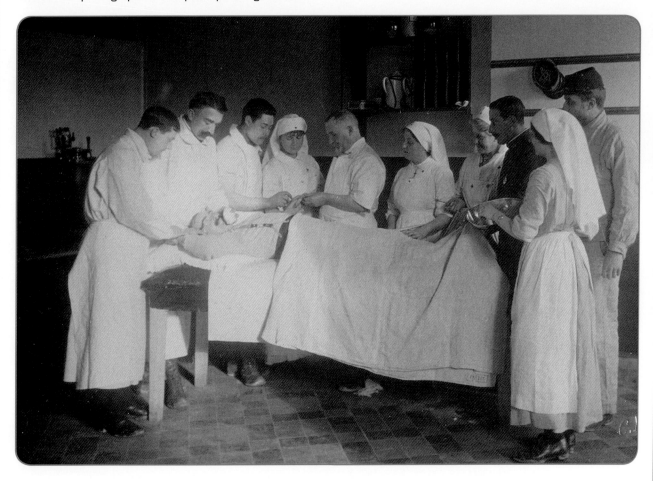

Source C: A description of the effect of Professor von Nussbaum using Lister's antiseptic ideas in a Munich hospital, from *The Early History of Surgery* by W. J. Bishop, 1962.

At his hospital in 1872, 80% of all wounds were affected by pyaemia and gangrene [septic infections]. And the death rate was horrifying. The antiseptic method was introduced and within a week von Nussbaum was able to report: 'Not another case of hospital gangrene appeared.'

Source D: An extract from Lister's records of the percentages of deaths from the amputations done while he was Professor of Surgery at Glasgow University.

Year	Total cases	Number of recoveries	Number of deaths	% deaths
1864–66 No antiseptics	35	19	16	45.7
1867–70 Antiseptics used	40	34	6	15.0

Source E: From *A Time to Heal*, by Jerry L. Gaw, 1999.

> One of the most heated debates concerned the practicality of the carbolic spray. Christopher Heath of University College Hospital referred to the spray as 'repellent' and said, 'Each time I use it I am nearly decided not to do it again.' Richard Barwell of Charing Cross Hospital argued that surgeons would not use Lister's technique, no matter how beneficial it was, if they found the process to be repellent.

Source F: From the modern website of the Australasian College of Surgeons.

> Lister's steam spray came to be used all over the world. However, it had serious disadvantages, which even Lister acknowledged. The main problem was the inhalation of carbolic vapour by everyone, including the patient and the operator. If the patient had been anaesthetised with chloroform, the gas lamps turned the vapour into chlorine gas [which burned the eyes, nose and throat and caused choking].

Source G: From *The Cambridge Illustrated History of Medicine* by Roy Porter, 2001.

> By 1900, antiseptic and aseptic methods were used by all surgeons. No longer did surgeons operate in blood-caked coats in dingy rooms with sawdust-covered floors. The introduction of face-masks, rubber gloves, and surgical gowns lessened the risks of infection and clean and sterile environments were constantly being improved.

The Unit 2 Exam

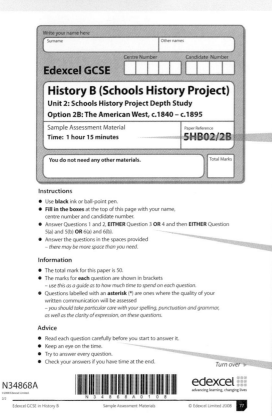

Edexcel GCSE

Write your name here

Surname | Other names

Centre Number | Candidate Number

History B (Schools History Project)
Unit 2: Schools History Project Depth Study
Option 2B: The American West, c.1840 – c.1895

Sample Assessment Material
Time: 1 hour 15 minutes

Paper Reference
5HB02/2B

You do not need any other materials.

Total Marks

Instructions
- Use **black** ink or ball-point pen.
- **Fill in the boxes** at the top of this page with your name, centre number and candidate number.
- Answer Questions 1 and 2, **EITHER** Question 3 **OR** 4 and then **EITHER** Question 5(a) and 5(b) **OR** 6(a) and 6(b).
- Answer the questions in the spaces provided
  – *there may be more space than you need.*

Information
- The total mark for this paper is 50.
- The marks for **each** question are shown in brackets
  – *use this as a guide as to how much time to spend on each question.*
- Questions labelled with an **asterisk** (*) are ones where the quality of your written communication will be assessed
  – *you should take particular care with your spelling, punctuation and grammar, as well as the clarity of expression, on these questions.*

Advice
- Read each question carefully before you start to answer it.
- Keep an eye on the time.
- Try to answer every question.
- Check your answers if you have time at the end.

Turn over ▶

N34868A
©2008 Edexcel Limited.
2/2

edexcel
advancing learning, changing lives

Edexcel GCSE in History B | Sample Assessment Materials | © Edexcel Limited 2008 | 77

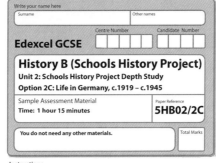

Edexcel GCSE

Write your name here

Surname | Other names

Centre Number | Candidate Number

History B (Schools History Project)
Unit 2: Schools History Project Depth Study
Option 2C: Life in Germany, c.1919 – c.1945

Sample Assessment Material
Time: 1 hour 15 minutes

Paper Reference
5HB02/2C

You do not need any other materials.

Total Marks

Instructions
- Use **black** ink or ball-point pen.
- **Fill in the boxes** at the top of this page with your name, centre number and candidate number.
- Answer Questions 1 and 2, **EITHER** Question 3 **OR** 4 and then **EITHER** Question 5(a) and 5(b) **OR** 6(a) and 6(b).
- Answer the questions in the spaces provided
  – *there may be more space than you need.*

Information
- The total mark for this paper is 50.
- The marks for **each** question are shown in brackets
  – *use this as a guide as to how much time to spend on each question.*
- Questions labelled with an **asterisk** (*) are ones where the quality of your written communication will be assessed
  – *you should take particular care with your spelling, punctuation and grammar, as well as the clarity of expression, on these questions.*

Advice
- Read each question carefully before you start to answer it.
- Keep an eye on the time.
- Try to answer every question.
- Check your answers if you have time at the end.

Turn over ▶

N35698A
©2008 Edexcel Limited.
2/2

edexcel
advancing learning, changing lives

Edexcel GCSE in History B | Sample Assessment Materials | © Edexcel Limited 2008 | 95

ResultsPlus
Watch out!

Don't just ignore the information on the front of the paper. Some of it is very helpful.

The most important part is, how long is the paper? In this case, it's 1 hour and 15 minutes. Keep your eye on the time throughout the exam, and **make sure you have enough time to answer the last question**, which is worth the most marks.

ResultsPlus
Top tip

There are six questions, and you must answer four of them. You choose between Question 3 and Question 4, and again between Question 5 and Question 6.

ResultsPlus
Top tip

This is all good advice. For this paper you should also study all the sources **before** you start answering the questions.

The Unit 2 Exam: A Depth Study

The Depth Study is a chance to study a short period (less than 60 years) in depth. You will have studied ONE of the following:

either   Unit 2A *The transformation of British society c1815–c1851*

or   Unit 2B *The American West c1840–c1895*.

or   Unit 2C *Life in Germany c1919–c1945*

The **structure of the examination** is the same for each. You will always have:

- **one examination paper** lasting **1 hour 15 minutes** in which you will write **five answers**.

The questions will always follow the pattern below.

The number of **marks** you can score for each question is given below.

So is the **time** the examiners recommend you spend on each question (with a few minutes spare for checking your answers).

Q1

4 marks	Question 1 will always give you a source to look at. Then it will ask you to **explain what you can learn about** [something] **from Source A**
6 minutes	

Q2

9 marks	Question 2 will ask you to choose one out of two people, groups, events or factors affecting them
12 minutes	**Choose one and explain their importance to** [something]

Q3 or 4

12 marks	Both Question 3 and Question 4 will ask you to ...
18 minutes	**analyse** something, giving a **description** and **explanation** of it

Q5 (a) or 6 (a)

9 marks	Both Question 5 (a) and Question 6 (a) will ask you to...
12 minutes	**Describe** or **explain** [something]

Q5 (b) or 6 (b)

16 marks	Both Question 5 (b) and Question 6 (b) will ask you to make and support a judgement. It might be in the form of a question such as:
25 minutes	**Was 'x' the most important cause of** [something]

To help you prepare for the examination, this book does three things.

- First, it helps you with **content**. There is a one-page overview of the content of your Unit. There are also **SuperFacts** for each part of the Unit. (SuperFacts are the key bits of information you need to answer the questions.)
- Secondly, it helps you with **questions**. It explains what you have to do to answer every type of question you will be asked and gives you a chance to test yourself.
- Thirdly, it helps you with **answers**. It provides model answers to all the questions, so you can see how you did.

Overview:
The American West c1840–c1895

People in the American West

INDIANS
Wanted:
- to keep their own way of life

Lifestyle:
- nomadic, following buffalo migration routes

Problems:
- whites taking land
- railways, farms and towns breaking up migration routes
- hostility of US army

Migration westward, and life in the West, helped by:
- US government
- US army
- railways

CATTLEMEN AND COWBOYS
Wanted:
- to make money from breeding and selling cattle

Lifestyle:
- semi-nomadic, ranches and cattle trails

Problems:
- homesteaders settling on trails
- cattle rustlers
- the weather

HOMESTEADERS
Wanted:
- to settle and farm

Lifestyle:
- settled, on farms

Problems:
- cattlemen wanting to cross their land
- not understanding how to farm the plains
- isolation
- the weather

THE MORMONS
Wanted:
- religious freedom

Lifestyle:
- settled, ruled by religious beliefs

Problems:
- beliefs led to clashes with government and non-Mormons

MINERS
Wanted:
- to find and claim gold

Lifestyle:
- semi-settled, but very basic, mostly male, wild settlements

Problems:
- lawlessness: claim jumping, theft and high levels of violence in the settlements

HOMESTEADERS AND CATTLEMEN
Set off by:
Cattlemen driving their herds over homesteaders' land and homesteaders putting up fences to stop this.

Resolved by:
Greater federal law enforcement. Ranchers settling down on smaller, fenced ranches after ranching became less profitable in the late 1880s.

TOWNSPEOPLE AND COWBOYS
Set off by:
Cow towns were mostly lawless at first. As families settled and the towns developed, townspeople did not want cowboys getting drunk, womanising and fighting when they came to town. The cowboys wanted to let off steam as they always had done at the end of the trail.

Resolved by:
Greater federal law enforcement. The drop in the number of cowboys (and the power of the ranchers) as ranching became less profitable in the late 1880s.

CONFLICT Different groups came into conflict in the west. For example ...

INDIANS AND SETTLERS
Set off by:
The various settlers' desire to own the land. Misunderstandings caused by the different beliefs and ways of life of the Indians and the whites (e.g. The US government made treaties with the Indians not understanding that Indians were not bound to obey the treaties their chiefs agreed to).

Resolved by:
The destruction of the Indian way of life. The whites (government, army and various settlers) took the land, killed the buffalo, broke up the tribes and forced the Indians to live on fixed reservations.

Section summary

The 13 states of the United States of America in 1783 were dotted along the Atlantic coast. But new states, further inland, were soon added. By 1840, the US government claimed almost all of the present-day United States. However, these lands had been occupied for many years by Native Americans. These people were not a single group, but many different groups. All had lifestyles and beliefs that were very different from those of the newly independent Americans.

People began to migrate westwards almost from the moment when the 13 states became independent. They went for various reasons: to farm, to set up towns, to practise their religion and to look for gold. Their reasons for going may have been different, but they almost all shared the assumption that they had the right to take land from the native peoples who already lived on it.

SuperFacts 1
Inhabitants and early settlers

SuperFacts are the key bits of information. Learn them and ask someone to test you.

The Great Spirit was the creator god of the Plains Indians. They saw nature and all living things as part of the Great Spirit, who gave everything (even rocks) a spirit. They believed in working with nature, not trying to alter it or own it. ●– p.6

Visions and dreams were important as contact with the spirit world. Visions were part of a child becoming an adult. All tribes had ceremonies for this. ●– p.6

Medicine men were a link to the spirit world, interpreting visions and dreams. They were also healers. Indians believed evil spirits caused illness by taking over a person. Healing combined prayer and herbal cures. ●– p.7–8

Plains Indians hunted buffalo and used every part of the animal but the heart (this was buried to keep the herd growing). Plains Indians were nomadic, following the buffalo across the Plains. Men hunted the buffalo; women and children cut it up. ●– p.8

Uses for buffalo parts included meat; shoes, clothes, bags, tipis, shields (hide); fuel (dung); food bags (bladder); knives, tools, sledges (bones); blankets, mittens, clothes (fur); hairbrushes (tongue); bowstrings, thread (sinews); soap (fat). ●– p.9

Horses made travel and hunting easier and changed the way Plains Indians fought. By the 1820s, Plains Indians measured wealth by horse ownership. ●– p.10

Tipis were circular homes, made of several buffalo hides wrapped around a framework of poles. Their conical shape resisted the wind that blew across the Plains. They were easy to take down and put up. ●– p.11

Plains Indians were nomads so had few possessions. Two of their tipi poles made a travois (sledge) for travel. Tribes had many bands, groups of people who were usually related (men sometimes got wives from other bands). ●– p.12

Living as a group Men hunted and protected the group. Women did all the other jobs. A man could have several wives. If a man died, another member of the group took the widow as his wife. Children, the tribe's future, were looked after by everyone. The old were looked after until too weak to travel. ●– p.12

Bands worked together Usually all the bands in a tribe met once a year in the summer. They traded horses and found wives. The bands and the tribes were led by a group of important men. But chiefs did not rule the tribe; they did not have to be obeyed. ●– p.13

The Sioux Nation was huge. It had seven tribes, each of which had smaller tribes (the Tetons had seven). Each smaller tribe had three to ten bands. ●– p.16

Warrior societies Every group had its own warrior society, made up of the best fighters. They worked with warrior societies from their tribe and fought others. They did not fight long battles about owning land. They held short raids on enemy tribes to capture horses or weapons, or avenge a wrong. ●– p.14

Beliefs about war Indians fought to show bravery and get horses or drive others away from buffalo hunting areas. They wanted to count coup to win status, not to kill. A warrior who killed an enemy scalped him to keep him from the afterlife. Scalps were dried and kept as trophies. ●– p.14

Migrants moved west, 'pushed' by poverty, unemployment or religious persecution. They were 'pulled' by cheap land (the price was set by government law, to encourage migration) and the hope of a better life, encouraged by tales of fertile land, lots of fish, lots of game animals and gold. ➡ p.18

Trappers were the earliest migrants. They hunted animals for fur. Some worked for big companies. Others, mountain men, worked for themselves. They were first to see and describe the fertile land over the Rocky Mountains and Sierra Nevada Mountains. ➡ p.18

Mountain men and Indians Some mountain men liked the Indian way of life. Jim Bridger married three Indians; Jim Beckwith lived with the Indians and even became a chief. Others, like Jeremiah Johnson, shot as many Indians as they could. Trappers brought alcohol, guns and various diseases with them. ➡ p.19

Jim Bridger and some other mountain men bought the Rocky Mountain Fur Company in 1830. The fur trade collapsed in the early 1840s (because of over-trapping) so he set up a trading post to sell supplies to Oregon Trail migrants. He led migrants along the trail and found the Bridger Pass that made it shorter. ➡ p.20

The Bridger Trail was set up by Jim Bridger in 1864. It was a safer route to the gold fields of Montana than the existing Bozeman Trail. ➡ p.20

Bridger and the army Jim Bridger worked as a guide for the US army as it moved west to fight the Indians who blocked the trails. ➡ p.20

Farmers moved west In 1837, an economic depression hit the USA. Banks closed (thousands of savers lost their money); wages dropped 40%; the price of crops fell. This pushed people to think of emigration. So did the rapid population rise in some places (e.g. Missouri: 14,000 in 1830; 353,000 in 1840). ➡ p.20

The first migrants failed to cross the Sierra Nevada in 1841 and 1842, but made it in 1843. They reached Oregon and California the following year. Soon there were several trails across the mountains; the most popular were the Oregon and California Trails. There were pamphlets describing the route. ➡ p.20

Danger on the trails Between 1840 and 1860, about 34,000 people died on the trails. The journey was long (the California Trail was 3,800 km and took from April to November or December). Supplies ran out; the weather was often bad; many trails involved crossing deserts; and Indians often attacked. ➡ p.20

Independence, Missouri was where migrants formed groups heading west. Travelling in groups meant people could help get wagons over mountains and through rivers. They could hunt together and keep watch against attack. ➡ p.20

The Donner Party In 1846, a group of 87 people followed a new route from a pamphlet. Wagons broke down in the desert, 300 of their cattle died. They got to Sierra Nevada late. The snow came early, trapping them in the mountains. Food ran out; starvation set in. A group went for help. Both groups ate their dead to survive. They were found in January 1847; 39 of the group had died. ➡ p.21

---

edexcel ⠿ **key terms**

counting coup An act of bravery in battle, when an Indian touched an enemy (or his horse) with his hand, a weapon, or a specially decorated 'coup stick'.

federal In the context of US government and this book, to do with the government that makes the laws for all of the USA. Each state can also make its own laws that only apply within the state.

Great Spirit The Plains Indians believed the Great Spirit created the world and ruled it.

scalping Making a circular cut on the top of the head and tearing off the hair and the skin below it.

sweat lodge A tipi which was heated by a fire. Plains Indians, usually just men, went there to purify themselves and, often, to have visions. Using a sweat lodge was often part of a longer religious ceremony.

visions Things that people believe they see. These things are not real, but they have a special significance to the person who 'sees' them.

Need more help?
You can find a longer explanation of each SuperFact in your Edexcel textbook, *The American West c1840–c1895*. Look for this symbol ➡, which will give you the page number.

ResultsPlus
Top tip

Read the question carefully and stick to the focus of the question. If you are asked 'Why were there problems of law and order in the mining towns in the far west in the **1850s and 1860s**?' you will not get any marks for discussing any problems before or after that date, however accurately you do so. So, discuss the discovery of gold, the rapid growth of these towns and the fact they were mostly inhabited by men (not families) who wanted to get rich quick. Discuss how their circumstances made the men drink, use prostitutes and fight and how the lack of a law enforcement system and town organisation meant force was the only law.

In 1848, gold was found in California Within months, 40,000 men were heading west overland, and 60 ships sailed west (from America and Europe). By the end of 1948, there were 10,000 miners. By the end of 1849, there were 90,000. Gold was later found in other places including Dakota (1874). ● p.23

Early mining towns had few families. The men had small shelters with no sanitation; there was a lot of disease. Towns grew fast, but had no local government. People 'claimed' an area of land to mine. Claim-jumping was common. There was a lot of crime. ● p.24

Later mining towns had more families living in them. They had better houses, streets and businesses. They chose officials to run the town, including sheriffs to arrest criminals. They set up courts to hold trials. Sometimes they also made up vigilante groups to break up gangs. ● p.24

Effects of the gold rush Californian cities grew quickly; the wealth generated by the gold rush boosted all US trade; people invested money in the West; there were huge numbers of migrants to the West. ● p.25

Problems of the gold rush Taxes on foreign miners and persecution (especially of the Chinese) caused trouble between different groups of settlers. The native Indians of California were almost wiped out. ● p.25

The Mormons (Church of the Latter Day Saints) were a religious group set up by Joseph Smith in New York State in 1823. By 1830, the church had several hundred members. Many people objected to their beliefs, which included the Book of Mormon replacing the Bible and polygamy. ● p.25

The Mormons moved on from New York State to Ohio (1831–37), Missouri (1837–38) and Illinois (1838–46). They were driven out by local dislike of their religious practices and, in Missouri, the fact that they had their own police (the Danites) and were friendly to Indians. ● p.25–26

Brigham Young led the Mormons west from Illinois. There were about 1,500 Mormons and they went to the Great Salt Lake, land no one wanted. Young organised the 2,250 km trip carefully. People travelled in small groups, with set tasks and a clearly set-out route. ● p.26

Salt Lake The first Mormons reached the salt flats around Salt Lake in August 1847. The lake was salty, but the streams that fed it were not. Young decided to stay there rather than move to more fertile land that people might want to take. Over the years, more and more Mormons came to Salt Lake. ● p.26

Young and Salt Lake City Young decided all the land was to belong to the Church and be given out fairly. Young then spread out across Utah. He had all the land around surveyed and, where farming was possible, set up towns, sending people with the right balance of skills to live in them. ● p.28

A planned city The Temple of Salt Lake City was in a square at the centre of the city. Roads were wide; plots of land were of fixed sizes. Family plots were 10–80 acres, depending on family size. Mechanics and other skilled workers (with less time to farm) had 5-acre plots. ● p.28

More Mormons Young set up a Perpetual Emigration Fund to pay for poor Mormons to immigrate to Utah. Mormons even came from Europe (e.g. 32,894 had left England by 1851). Young wanted to be able to push the government to make the Mormons politically independent. ● p.28

In 1848 Young asked for independence The government said Utah could run its own affairs but had to follow federal laws and accept non-Mormon settlers. However, Young was governor so the Danites began imposing Mormon control, despite the law. In 1857 a non-Mormon governor (with 1,500 soldiers) took over. ● p.29

1857 massacre In 1857, there was a massacre of migrants. The Mormons blamed the Indians; some migrants blamed the Mormons. The government tightened its control. It only allowed Utah to become a state after the Mormons accepted a non-Mormon governor and polygamy was banned in 1890. ● p.29

Dividing the land in the West At first, the government surveyed the land in the West and divided it into townships of about 10 square kilometres. These were split into 640-acre plots sold at $1 an acre to help settlers – but the plots were still too big and expensive. ● p.35

The Homestead Act (1862) said people could claim 160 acres, which was officially registered. After 5 years, they could pay $30 for a certificate of ownership. The Timber and Culture Act of 1873 allowed people to claim another 160 acres if they planted trees on half of it. ● p.35

Railroad companies In 1869, the Union Pacific and Central Pacific railroad companies finished the first railroad across the Great Plains. By 1893, there were six. The various railway companies owned about 155 million acres on the Plains, much of which they sold off to encourage towns to grow. ● p.35

Problems faced by homesteaders Breaking new ground: grass roots 10 cm deep bent iron ploughs. Lack of water (38 cm of rain a year, in summer, so some evaporated). Fire (grass very dry in summer and autumn). The wrong crops (e.g. wheat). Animal pests (e.g. straying cattle, grasshoppers 1874–77). ● p.39–40

Technological solutions to problems Steel ploughs and more machinery (made cheaper by mass-production); wells (drilled very deep with a high-powered drill) and wind pumps (for a steady supply of water); railroads (brought supplies); barbed wire (fenced the land, kept cattle off crops). ● p.41

Other solutions to problems Dry-farming techniques; using 'Turkey Red' wheat (brought over in 1874 by Russian migrants) which was more suited to the climate. ● p.42

Women helped to build the home (mostly from blocks of earth). There was little wood; women collected dried cow and buffalo dung for fuel. They helped farm. They cooked, cleaned and made the family's clothes. They nursed the sick, had children and brought them up. ● p.38

Community life built up slowly. Farms were big and families were isolated. But townships slowly grew (even employing teachers) and neighbours helped each other. Women met up to sew quilts together. They helped each other preserved food. They helped each other in childbirth. Neighbours met up for picnics and holiday celebrations. ● p.38–39

Results Plus
Watch out!

The textbook, and the SuperFacts, give you useful generalisations. But generalising makes all people seem the same, which they are not, and never have been.

When answering exam questions, make sure that you show the examiner that you know that not everyone was the same in the past and that not all Plains Indians felt the same about settlers, for example. Use 'most', 'some' or 'usually' to qualify generalisations.

Need more help?
You can find a longer explanation of each SuperFact in your Edexcel textbook, *The American West c1840–c1895*. Look for this symbol ●, which will give you the page number.

Section summary

After 1860, life in the American West changed rapidly. The government encouraged migration and the railroads that brought more settlers, supplies and new technology to help homesteaders farm more efficiently.

The cattle boom lasted from 1867 to 1885. In the mid-1860s cattle were driven to the nearest railroad, then taken north for sale. Later, they were sold at cow towns in the West. Between 1880–85, ranchers raised cattle on huge 'open ranches' on the Plains. After the winter of 1886 wiped out about 15% of the cattle on the Plains, many ranchers changed to running smaller, fenced ranches.

Law and order was a problem in the West. There were many different groups, all with different needs. The US army dealt with problems with the Indians, but not with other aspects of law and order. There was trouble between ranchers and homesteaders over land. There was conflict between cowboys and people in towns, between ranchers and farmers and between whites and Chinese. Federal justice was not effective. Once separate states emerged, they ran their own justice systems.

SuperFacts 2
Development of the Plains

SuperFacts are the key bits of information. Learn them and ask someone to test you.

Coast-to-coast railroads In 1850 there were about 200,000 km of railroads; none were west of the Mississippi and Missouri rivers. In 1890, there were over 340,000 km of track – most of the new track was in the West. ●– p.50

The government wanted railroads to make trade links with countries from the west coast (e.g. with China); to help migrants travel west more easily and to get supplies; to unite the nation; to give the government more control over the West. ●– p.49

The Pacific Railways Act (1862) set up two railroad companies: the Union Pacific and the Central Pacific. Union Pacific laid track from the Missouri River west across the Plains. Central Pacific went east from Sacramento. They met in Utah in May 1869 and joined the lines with a golden spike. ●– p.49

Railroad land The government gave railroad companies land to build on, all along the tracks. It was hard to find workers. Central Pacific hired Chinese workers. In 1868, two-thirds of its 4,000 workers were Chinese. ●– p.49

Problems of construction included crossing mountains, valleys, deserts; the weather; poor living conditions (hundreds of workers died); worker shortage (Central Pacific needed 5,000 workers; in 1864 it had just 600); Indian attacks. ●– p.49

Impact on settlers The railways brought: government law enforcement; farm machinery; supplies of all kinds (e.g. clothes, pots, lamps) and the chance to open ports to trade with the Far East. Railways took cattle and crops east. Towns and cities grew (and grew more civilised) as travel and transport were easier. ●– p.51

Impact on the Plains Indians The railroads crossed hunting grounds and buffalo migration routes. Homesteaders fenced land they saw as theirs; the Indians believed you did not own land. White settlers hunted buffalo for sport. They killed the buffalo and left them to rot, or just used the hides, not the rest of the animal. ●– p.52

The Central Pacific (left) and Union Pacific (right) lines meet on 10 May 1869.

Early cattle trails As the US population grew, demand for meat grew faster. Texas cowboys set up trails to drive cattle to markets (e.g. New Orleans, Chicago). Some cattlemen built ranches near the trails to raise cattle. ●▬ p.55

The Civil War (1861–65) Texas ranchers and cowboys went to fight and came back to find 5 million cattle roaming wild. They rounded them up and began 'cattle drives' north (where cattle sold for $40–$50 each against $4–$5 in Texas). ●▬ p.55

Cattle trains Railroads helped the cattle industry grow. Ranchers did not have to drive their cattle so far. They went north to the first east/west railroad. Railway companies organised refrigerated cattle trains to St Louis then on to Chicago. ●▬ p.55

Charles Goodnight was a Texas rancher who set up the Goodnight–Loving Trail with Oliver Loving, a cattle drover. They took cattle to Fort Sumner, to feed the army at the fort and also the Indians put in a reservation by the army. ●▬ p.55

Cattle trail problems included attacks by Indians; homesteaders whose land they drove cattle over (fearing damage and cattle ticks); rustlers who wanted to steal the cattle; feeding the cattle (they lost weight, many died). ●▬ p.56

Joseph McCoy set up Abilene, the first cow town in the West. Ranchers and buyers from the north met there, by the railroad. It had a lot of cattle pens, good grassland for grazing, a few houses and a small hotel. The first cattle arrived in 1867. From 1867 to 1881, nearly 1.5 million cattle were sold there. ●▬ p.56

Moving west As the newer railways moved west (Missouri Pacific; Atchison, Topeka and Santa Fe; Kansas Pacific) so did the cow towns (e.g. Dodge City, Newton). New trails were made to these towns, which had an economic boom (they handled nearly 4 million cattle from 1867 to 1885). ●▬ p.56

Getting rich People in cow towns made money: the ranchers; the cattle dealers who set up the towns (who took a fee on all sales); people with businesses in the towns (hotels, saloons). ●▬ p.56

John Iliff had the first big ranch on the Plains. He bought cattle and bred them for taste: refrigerated rail trucks meant cattle could be sent north as meat. He sold meat to railroad-building workers and a large Sioux Indian settlement. ●▬ p.57

Homesteaders versus cattlemen The railroads brought many homesteaders, given land by the government. At first, some ranchers just drove their cattle across the land, on the old trail. The homesteaders fenced their farms, often with barbed wire. Trails were blocked by homesteads. Some cattlemen cut the wire and drove their cattle over the land anyway. ●▬ p.57

edexcel ⠿ key terms

cattle ticks Bugs that bite cattle and other animals with hooves. At best, they mark the skins. But, if the infection isn't stopped, they cause starvation and death.

cowboys Workers hired to round up cattle, brand them and either drive them on the cattle trails or (when there were ranches on the Plains) to the nearest railroad or slaughterhouse.

head Cattle, and other animals, are sometimes referred to as 'head'. So 36,000 head of cattle is 36,000 animals.

Need more help?
You can find a longer explanation of each SuperFact in your Edexcel textbook, *The American West c1840–c1895*. Look for this symbol ●▬, which will give you the page number.

edexcel ⠿ key terms

cattle drovers People who organised trail drives and sometimes made their own trails.

rustlers People who steal cattle or other herd animals (e.g. sheep).

stampede When a herd of cattle gets scared and runs off, out of control.

ResultsPlus
Top tip

When asked about the importance of an event, or what difficulties or problems different groups faced, make sure you give relevant detail to back up what you say **and** link that detail to the focus of the question.

For example, if asked to describe the difficulties faced by migrants travelling west by wagon train in the 1840s, you must focus on the specific group (migrants travelling on wagon trains) and the specific date (the 1840s). You will not be rewarded for discussing difficulties of the cattle trail, or farming on the Plains, no matter how accurately. Nor will you be rewarded for discussing rail travel or wagon trails outside the 1840s. Discuss the problems presented by the mountains, the weather, the length of the journey, the cost, the need to know the route and the problems of supplies and Indian attacks.

Ranching on the Plains became a better option after 1880. It avoided clashes with homesteaders and Indians. Cattle weren't driven as far, so stayed fatter, fewer died than on the trail. The peak ranching years were 1880–85. ● p.57

Plains ranches were open range Ranchers didn't own or fence the land. They claimed the right to graze and make a water supply. Ranches were huge, so cattle were branded to show who owned them. ● p.57

Cattle on the Plains In 1860, Kansas had 93,000 cattle; in 1880 it had 1,500,000. In 1860, Colorado had none; in 1880 it had 800,000. In 1860, Montana had none; in 1880 it had 423,000. ● p.57

Boom to bust Since the 1860s, cattlemen (by running trails or ranching) had made more and more money. But as prices rose, ranchers bred too many cattle. This had two effects: there wasn't enough grass (made worse by the 1883 drought) and meat prices fell because so much was produced. ● p.58

The winter of 1886 followed a cold winter and a hot dry summer. The grazing and price problems forced some ranchers to sell up. Those who stayed faced temperatures as low as -55 °C. At least 15% of all cattle on the Plains died, as did many cowboys. Many ranchers went bankrupt. ● p.58

Ranching changed After 1886, ranchers built smaller, fenced ranches (made cattle easier to find in bad weather). They bred fewer cattle (kept prices up). They used new technology (e.g. barbed wire, portable wind pumps). ● p.58

Cowboys were mostly young men (black, white, Mexican, Indian). Some were ex-Civil War soldiers or criminals. Few cowboys had families. ● p.59

Cowboys on the trail were usually hired in spring to get the cattle to the end of the trail. They rounded up, branded and drove the cattle (their boss', or several herds; the trail of cattle could stretch over 2 km). They started fast, then moved at 20 km a day, to graze the cattle. When they arrived, their job was over. ● p.59–60

Dangers of the trail included stampedes (especially in the first days of the drive); natural dangers (wolves, scorpions, snakes); crossing rivers and quicksand; attacks by hostile Indian groups (not all were hostile); rustlers. ● p.60

Cowboys on ranches had full-time jobs, bunkhouses to sleep in and meals from a cookhouse. They rode ranch boundaries, checking no one was using the land and looking for sick or injured animals. Some found ranch life difficult after the free life of the trail; many bosses banned alcohol, knives and guns. ● p.60

Law and order in the West was hard for the government to enforce because: it was far away (from both law and government); mining and cow towns grew fast, had little organisation and a mainly male population (many ex-soldiers and criminals) given to drinking, hiring prostitutes and fighting. ● p.62

Conflict was likely between homesteaders and ranchers, between different ethnic groups and between cowboys and townspeople. Early mining and cow towns had no law and order system, force ruled. ●▬ p.62

Common crimes were cattle rustling; bank robberies (e.g. James Younger gang 1866–82); fence cutting (to get to water or cross fenced land); claim jumping (gold rush); trail robberies (train/stagecoach routes). ●▬ p.63–64

Other crimes (murder, racial crimes and theft) happened more often in the West; there was no law enforcement system at first, only local solutions (e.g. vigilantes). The army gave some protection near their forts. Stagecoach and railroad companies paid people to guard their travellers. ●▬ p.63–64

Violence in early cow towns, such as Dodge City, was common. Cowboys, after a long time on the trail, gambled, womanised and fought. As towns grew, town councils made rules about carrying guns. From 1870 to 1885, only 39 men died from gunshot wounds. In 1872, Abilene banned cowboys. ●▬ p.64

Vigilante committees were the first law and order solution in early towns. They caught criminals and either lynched them or ran them out of town. Later a local/federal system developed (see *Top tip* box). Finally, when an area became a state it could make its own laws and run its own justice system. ●▬ p.66

Jesse James and his brother, Frank, ran a gang that robbed banks, trains and stagecoaches in several states. In 1881, townspeople fought back. Jesse and Frank survived, went on the run and then set up another gang. Jesse was shot by a gang member tempted by the $10,000 reward offered by the governor. ●▬ p.65

Wyatt Earp was a law enforcer who lost his job several times for breaking the law (sheriffs were sometimes dishonest). In 1879, he and his brothers became 'the law' in Tombstone. Disputes with local families (Clantons and McLaurys) ended in a gunfight at the OK Corral. The Earps won, but had to flee. ●▬ p.68

The Johnson County War (Wyoming, 1892) was started by the Wyoming Stock Growers' Association (big ranchers). When homesteaders took on land from bankrupt ranchers and fenced it, disputes began. In 1892, the Stock Growers said homesteaders and small ranchers were rustling their cattle. ●▬ p.68

Albert Bothwell, a rancher, suspected the local storeowners of rustling. He and his friends lynched them; more violence followed. The Stock Growers hired gunmen, made a list of suspects and made a plan to capture the town of Buffalo and to kill the sheriff and everyone on the list. ●▬ p.69

The invasion, April 1892 The governor approved the invasion; reporters covered it. The sheriff heard of it and sent for the army. He and 300 men held off the invaders until the US Cavalry arrived. The invaders were arrested and tried, but never convicted. ●▬ p.70

ResultsPlus
Watch out!

Make sure you know the structure of US law enforcement that grew up.

Towns appointed:
Sheriffs (for 2 years)
Marshals (for 1 year).
They dealt with law and order in the town.

The federal government appointed:
US marshals and deputy marshals
They dealt with law and order in a state or territory in that state. They covered a big area, so had deputies to cover specific towns or parts of the countryside.

Federal judges
They toured a large area, holding trials of all criminals arrested since their last visit. There were long gaps between visits; local people sometimes took matters into their own hands.

Need more help?
You can find a longer explanation of each SuperFact in your Edexcel textbook, *The American West c1840–c1895*. Look for this symbol ●▬, which will give you the page number.

Section summary

As soon as settlers moved onto the Plains there was conflict with the Indians who already lived there. The groups had very different cultures, a very different approach to living and the land. Very few people on either side could understand the other group.

In 1832, the US government set up the Bureau of Indian Affairs to run the land they had decided to 'give' to the Indians. But, as more and more whites moved onto the Plains (and as gold and silver were discovered in various parts of the West), the government view of what to 'give' changed. So did their attitude to the Indians. At first, they tried to negotiate with the Indians, but, after the late 1860s, they shifted to a policy of forcing the Indians onto government-run reservations and destroying their old way of life.

SuperFacts 3
Conflict of the Plains

SuperFacts are the key bits of information. Learn them and ask someone to test you.

The 95th meridian was, from the 1830s, the US government's dividing line between white and Indian lands – the Permanent Indian Frontier. It took no account of hunting grounds or the Indian idea that land could not be owned. ● p.74

Early treaties In 1849, treaties with several Indian tribes (including the Plains Comanche and Kiowa) promised land west of the line, if the Indians left travellers alone; the area was to be one big Indian 'reservation'. ● p.76

Chiefs were not rulers If they agreed a treaty it didn't mean all their people were bound to obey it. This was something the US government and most white settlers did not understand. ● p.76

The Fort Laramie Treaty (1851) between the Cheyenne, the Arapaho and the government gave the Indians land below the Rocky Mountains, protection and $50,000 a year for 10 years. The tribes promised to allow US forts on the land and to stop attacking the Oregon Trail. The idea of a single reservation and a permanent frontier between Indians and whites was abandoned. ● p.76

Gold was found in the Rocky Mountains in 1859. White men crossed Indian land to get there; the railroads crossed it; settlers began to move onto it. They ignored the fact that some of this land was sacred burial ground and some crossed buffalo migration routes. In return, Indians began attacking railway surveyors and travellers. ● p.77

The Fort Wise Treaty (1861), forced on the chiefs, took away the land given at Fort Laramie. It set up a smaller reservation. Many warriors rejected it. They retaliated with raids on mining camps and attacks on mail coaches. ● p.77

Fort Laramie in 1849. In times of peace, Indians came to trade at the forts.

The Indian Wars (1862–76) The army and various Indian tribes fought, made agreements and fought again. Both sides hoped to negotiate a peace, both sides broke negotiated treaties. ●▶ p.78

Little Crow's War (1862) In 1861, the Santee Sioux reservation's crops failed. The Agency did not help. People starved. In August 1862, Little Crow and his warriors attacked the Agency and took food, killing soldiers sent to stop them. More troops came and, by October, the Indians were beaten and sent to a smaller reservation on barren land. ●▶ p.78

Sand Creek Massacre (1864) The Cheyenne in Sand Creek, Colorado, raided wagon trains for food when starving in 1862. They left migrants unharmed, but raided well into 1864. Black Kettle, the chief, met with government officials and the army. The army massacred his camp, over 450 people. ●▶ p.78

Reaction to Sand Creek Chief Black Kettle escaped and told of the attack. Whites and Indians were shocked at the massacre of men, women and children, some waving the white flag of truce. Peace was made with the remaining Cheyenne, who moved to an Oklahoma reservation. ●▶ p.79

Red Cloud's War (1865–68) Red Cloud of the Lakota Sioux attacked migrants on the Bozeman Trail, heading for the Montana gold fields. In 1866 the government set up talks, but Red Cloud left when he heard the army planned two more forts on the trail. He held talks with other Sioux tribes. ●▶ p.79

Red Cloud's success Red Cloud joined up with Sioux led by Sitting Bull and Crazy Horse. Some other tribes joined him, too. He kept them fighting in the winter (this was not their custom). In December 1866 they surrounded Fort Kearney, holding up Bozeman Trail traffic. The Indians kept on raiding. ●▶ p.79

The Fort Laramie Treaty (1868) The US government abandoned the forts and the Bozeman Trail. Red Cloud agreed to move to a reservation in Dakota. The government moved to a policy of many small Indian reservations. ●▶ p.80

The Great Sioux War (1876–77) The peace of 1868 broke down when the Fort Laramie Treaty was broken by the Northern Pacific railroad crossing Indian land (including sacred burial grounds and buffalo migration routes). Prospectors rushed in to stake their claim to the gold found by General Custer and the 8th Cavalry in 1874. ●▶ p.80

The government offered to buy the Black Hills for $6 million. The Indians refused, so, in December 1875, the government gave them 60 days to leave the reservation. It was impossible to do so in the deep snow of winter. ●▶ p.80

edexcel ⦙⦙⦙ key terms

reservations (in the context of this book) Areas of land set aside for different tribes to live on.

Agencies (in the context of this book) Indian Agencies set up by the Bureau of Indian Affairs to run the reservations.

ResultsPlus
Top tip

Make sure you understand the different ideas about war held by Indians and whites. It caused a lot of problems because, when they fought, each side had different 'rules' of war. So US soldiers thought the Indians were cowardly for their use of traditional raiding tactics and their preference to 'count coup' instead of killing. They were trained to fight set battles out in the open and kill as many of the enemy as they could.

Need more help?
You can find a longer explanation of each SuperFact in your Edexcel textbook, *The American West c1840–c1895*. Look for this symbol ●▶, which will give you the page number.

War By spring 1876, over 7,000 Indians (2,000 of them warriors) were ready for war. Sitting Bull and Crazy Horse wiped out an army camp near their own camp, then moved west towards a river they called Little Big Horn. ●─ p.80

Custer attacked the Sioux camp at Little Big Horn on 25 June 1876, despite having only 600 men against over 2,000 warriors and not enough bullets. He split his troops and ended up fighting with just 255 men. There are conflicting stories about the battle but, after about an hour, Custer and his men were dead. ●─ p.81

The Battle of Little Big Horn changed government policy towards the Indians. Public pressure to wipe out the Indians was enormous. The government, army and railroads all helped to destroy the Indian way of life. The government's role was important because it changed the policy and supplied the army. ●─ p.84

The army always saw the Indians as the enemy, even when the government wanted to negotiate. Their 'total war' policy meant attacking the whole tribe, not just the warriors (e.g. to force them onto the reservations they attacked and destroyed all their tipis, belongings and animals). ●─ p.85

Disadvantages The army had far fewer men than the Indians. They had to cover huge areas of the Plains, where they were often lost and could not live as the Indians did. They were trained to fight wars and big battles; not short sharp raids. Most were infantry; the Indians fought on horseback. ●─ p.85

Using enemies The army recruited spies (called scouts) from tribes that were hostile to the Sioux, to find out about Sioux tactics, migration and weapons. These Indians also became the enemy when no longer useful. ●─ p.86

Weapons were vital to the army's success. Indians traditionally fought with bows and arrows, clubs, spears and knives. Once they started to fight whites, they began to collect guns, but the army had far more guns and a wider range, including Gatling guns (early machine guns). ●─ p.86

Forts were useful to the army. They provided warm, safe bases for winter attacks on the Indians, who did not like to fight in bad weather. Heavy snow and freezing temperatures weakened their ability to fight. The army could use the railroads for transport. ●─ p.86

The railroads built track across buffalo migration routes and land that was sacred to the Indians. They brought homesteaders, the US army and buffalo hunters onto the Plains. They helped the cattle industry grow by transporting cattle (then meat) north and east and bringing supplies back. ●─ p.87

The government encouraged migration and the railroads. It made treaties with the Indians and broke them; always taking more land from the Indians and forcing them to settle on reservations. It even gave away land (e.g. 2 million acres in the Oklahoma land race, 1889) to encourage migration. ●─ p.88

The Dawes Act (1887) The Dawes General Allotment Act divided all Indian reservations into farms. Any land left was sold to white settlers. Many Indians didn't want to settle and farm. They refused the land or sold it to whites at too low a price and became homeless. ●– p.87

Reservations were set up to keep Indians and whites apart. Government Indian agents who ran the reservations were often corrupt, providing no medical care and little food. Sitting Bull didn't cooperate, but other chiefs did. Some Indians settled; some even joined the Indian Agency police. ●– p.92–93

Government control The government replaced chiefs with Indian councils and courts. These were abolished in 1885 and replaced by US federal law courts. Indians were no longer allowed to govern themselves. They could not migrate or hunt buffalo. Their old skills had no value on reservations. ●– p.92

Indian children were sent to boarding schools (over 2,000 children by 1887) or day schools (about 2,500 children by 1887) to unlearn Indian ways. ●– p.92

Religion The government banned all Indian feasts, ceremonies and dances on reservations. Instead, they sent Christian missionaries to 'civilise' them. ●– p.94

Industry's impact Demand for buffalo hides went up sharply in 1871, when a way was found to make good leather from them. Buffalo were wiped out on the southern Plains by 1875; on the northern Plains (following the arrival of the Northern Pacific Railroad and the defeat of the Sioux) by 1883. ●– p.94

The government wanted Indians on reservations, farming, not roaming the Plains hunting buffalo. They encouraged whites to hunt the buffalo to extinction, to force the Indians onto the reservations and make them change their way of life. ●– p.95

The Ghost Dance In 1890, a young Indian said he had had a vision: if all Indians danced (and kept on dancing) the Great Spirit would bring all dead Indians back to life to carry the whites away. ●– p.96

Sitting Bull supported ghost dances More and more Indians began to dance. Many dancers believed that shirts worn to ghost dance kept the dancer safe from bullets or white attacks. Some dancers waved rifles as they danced, and whites felt more and more threatened. ●– p.96

Sitting Bull was shot when the US army moved in to stop the ghost dances. Another chief, Big Foot, left his reservation with 120 men and 230 women and children. It was December and the snow slowed them down. The army caught up with them. ●– p.96

Battle of Wounded Knee (29 December 1890) The army caught Big Foot's group and took them to a place called Wounded Knee. The army began to disarm them; the Indians began to dance. Shooting broke out. Ten minutes later, 250 Indians and 25 soldiers lay dead; Indian resistance ended. ●– p.96

Need more help?
You can find a longer explanation of each SuperFact in your Edexcel textbook, *The American West c1840–c1895*. Look for this symbol ●–, which will give you the page number.

Top tip

An **inference** is a judgement made from the source, which is not directly stated by it.

A **supported** inference is one that uses detail from the source to prove the inference.

Consider this example:

Source A: 'Sue pushed her friend, Liz, off the swing. Liz's mother was angry and said she was going to tell Sue's mother what had happened.'

Question: *What does Source A tell us about Sue?*

Information: *Source A tells us Sue pushed Liz off the swing.* [This is directly stated in the source, so it's not an inference.]

An inference could be: *Source A tells me that Sue is in serious trouble and is likely to be punished.* [The source does not directly tell us this, but we can infer that it is likely.]

A supported inference could be: *Source A tells me Sue is in serious trouble and likely to be punished. I can infer this because she pushed Liz off the swing and Liz's mum was cross and was going to tell Sue's mum, who would be cross too.* [An inference, with supporting details quoted from the source.]

Top tip

When you are asked what you can learn from a source, make sure you do not just describe the source. To get the best marks you have to make an inference from the source, work out something extra from it. You must also tell the examiner what part of the source led you to make the inference.

Answering questions: Question 1

What you need to do

Question 1 will always ask:

> **What can you learn from Source A about... [something]?**

The best answers:
- make **inferences** from the source [*see Top tip box*]
- and **support** those inferences with detail from the source.

Here is a **source** and a **question** for you to study.

Source A: A photograph of a Cheyenne Indian family and their tipi.

What can you learn from Source A about Indian lifestyle?

(i) Write the inference you can make from the supporting detail provided.

(ii) Write the supporting detail that goes with the inference provided.

Inference	Supporting detail
One thing I can infer from Source A is that ... [i]	I can infer this because the source shows that the family have no permanent house, only a tipi which could be easily taken down and then moved.
I can also infer from Source A that living in tipis was very cramped.	I can infer this because ... [ii]

An answer like this, with **two** inferences, both **supported by detail** in the source would gain full marks.

Answering questions: Question 2

Question 2 will always show you two people, two groups of people, or factors or events.

It will then say:

> *Choose one and explain the importance of this person/group/factor/event for...*
> *[something]*

What you need to do

The best answers will not just write all they know about the person, group, factor or event, but will instead:

- say what the importance of the person (or group, factor or event) was

- give supporting detail about their actions to explain how the person (or group, factor or event) was important.

How you do it

Take this question as an example:

> *The boxes below show two people. Choose one and explain the importance of that person to the US cattle industry 1860–80.*

Charles Goodnight

Joseph McCoy

Let's choose to write our answer about **Joseph McCoy**.

We will use the SuperFacts on the right in our answer. Remember the focus of the question, the **importance** of McCoy. Remember to provide **supporting detail** for what you say.

Importance	Supporting Detail
Joseph McCoy was important to the cattle industry because he found a way to overcome the problems of the cattle trails.	For example, McCoy set up the town of Abilene, the first cow town in the West. Ranchers and buyers could meet there by the railway. From 1867–81 1.5 million cattle were sold there. Other people copied him, setting up cow towns like Denver and Newton. Everyone made money: the ranchers, the cattle dealers and business owners in the towns. So McCoy helped the cattle industry to become very prosperous.

An answer like this, which states the **importance** of the person and gives **detail** to **explain** it, will reach the top level.

The best answers may be longer than this one, but they must follow this pattern.

Now turn the page to practise this yourself.

SuperFacts

Joseph McCoy set up Abilene, the first cow town in the West. Ranchers and buyers from the north met there, by the railroad. It had a lot of cattle pens, good grassland for grazing, a few houses and a small hotel. The first cattle arrived in 1867. From 1867 to 1881, nearly 1.5 million cattle were sold there.

Moving west As the newer railways moved west (Missouri Pacific; Atchison, Topeka and Santa Fe; Kansas Pacific) so did the cow towns (e.g. Dodge City, Newton). New trails were made to these towns, which had an economic boom (they handled nearly 4 million cattle from 1867 to 1885).

Getting rich People in cow towns made money: the ranchers; the cattle dealers who set up the towns (who took a fee on all sales); people with businesses in the towns (hotels, saloons).

The answer
You can find suggested answers to the tasks numbered (i), (ii), etc., on page 99.

SuperFacts

Jim Bridger and some other mountain men bought the Rocky Mountain Fur Company in 1830. The fur trade collapsed in the early 1840s (over-trapping) so he set up a trading post to sell supplies to Oregon Trail migrants. He led migrants along the trail and found the Bridger Pass that made it shorter.

The Bridger Trail was set up by Jim Bridger in 1864. It was a safer route to the gold fields of Montana than the existing Bozeman Trail.

Bridger and the army Jim Bridger worked as a guide for the US army as it moved west to fight the Indians who blocked the trails.

Brigham Young led the Mormons west from Illinois. There were about 1,500 Mormons and they went to the Great Salt Lake, land no one wanted. Young organised the 2,250km trip carefully. People travelled in small groups, with set tasks and a clearly set-out route.

Salt Lake The first Mormons reached the salt flats around Salt Lake in August 1847. The lake was salty, but the streams that fed it were not. Young decided to stay there rather than move to more fertile land that people might want to take. Over the years, more and more Mormons came to Salt Lake.

More Mormons Young set up a Perpetual Emigration Fund to pay for poor Mormons to immigrate to Utah. Mormons even came from Europe (e.g. 32,894 had left England by 1851). Young wanted to be able to push the government to make the Mormons politically independent.

The answer
You can find suggested answers to the tasks numbered (i), (ii), etc., on page 123.

Now test yourself
Here is another possible Question 2.

We will use the SuperFacts on the left in our answer.

The boxes below show two people. Choose one and explain his importance in the migration of settlers to the West.

> Jim Bridger

> Brigham Young

First, write an answer about **Jim Bridger** in the box below.

Importance	Supporting detail
Jim Bridger was important in the migration of settlers to the West because... (i)	For example, Bridger... (ii)

In the exam you must just choose **one** topic.

But, just for practice, write about **Brigham Young** in the boxes below.

This time, we haven't started you off with 'signpost' phrases. We've left you to write your own 'signposts' to show the examiner exactly how you are answering the question.

Importance	Supporting detail
(iii)	(iv)

Answering questions: Questions 3 and 4

In the exam, you have to answer **either** Question 3 **or** Question 4.

Questions 3 and 4 will always ask you to **analyse** something, describing and explaining it. For example, the questions may ask you why something happened.

The questions will then always give you some information to help you with your answer.

For example, Question 3 or 4 could say:

> *Why, despite being outnumbered, was the US army able to defeat the Indians in warfare?*

You may use the following in your answer and any other information of your own.
- The policy of 'total warfare' meant attacking the whole community, not just warriors.
- The army had rifles and bigger guns, such as Gatling guns.
- Forts provided warm, safe bases for winter attacks.

What you need to do

The best answers will:
- **state reasons** why the US army was successful
- after each reason, **give details to explain how** each reason helped them win.

You do not have to use the information given in the box under the question.

However, it is a good place to start.

How you do it

Take the question above as an example.

Use the SuperFact on this page and the next to help you.

We have used important, introductory words at the start of our answer. These words are 'signposts' which help the examiner see how you are answering the question.

You could start by using the first piece of information given in the question, like this.

> One reason why the US army was successful against the Indians was their use of 'total warfare'.

> The US army always saw the Indians as the enemy, even when the government wanted to negotiate. So they used 'total warfare'. This meant attacking the whole tribe, not just the warriors. For example, to force Indians onto the reservations the army attacked and destroyed all the Indian tipis, belongings and animals. So, using total warfare meant they could force the Indians to do what they wanted.

ResultsPlus
Top tip

Questions 3 and 4 will always be followed by some useful information to help you with your answer. This extra information could be useful information, a quote or a picture.

It will be useful and relevant information. You can use other information as long as it is **relevant to the focus of the question**. You do not need to do so.

Answers that are closely tied to the focus of the question, rather than talking around it, will reach the top level.

SuperFacts

The army always saw the Indians as the enemy, even when the government wanted to negotiate. Their 'total war' policy meant attacking the whole tribe, not just the warriors (e.g. to force them onto the reservations they attacked and destroyed all their tipis, belongings and animals).

SuperFacts

Using enemies The army recruited spies (called scouts) from tribes that were hostile to the Sioux, to find out about Sioux tactics, migration and weapons. These Indians also became the enemy when no longer useful.

Weapons were vital to the army's success. Indians traditionally fought with bows and arrows, clubs, spears and knives. Once they started to fight whites, they began to collect guns, but the army had far more guns and a wider range, including Gatling guns (early machine guns).

Forts were useful to the army. They provided warm, safe bases for winter attacks on the Indians, who did not like to fight in bad weather. Heavy snow and freezing temperatures weakened their ability to fight. The army could use the railroads for transport.

The answer
You can find suggested answers to the tasks numbered (i), (ii), etc., on page 123.

Now test yourself

We have used the first piece of extra information in the question to start the answer.

Now you use the second and third pieces of information in the question to finish it.

> Another reason why the US army were able to defeat the Indians in warfare was because they had better weapons. **Hint:** compare US army weapons with those of the Indians.

> (i)

> A third reason why the army was able to defeat the Indians in warfare was ... (ii)

> These were important because ... (iii)

Remember, you can add your **own reasons** to those given in the question.

- For example, in answer to this question, you could say:

> Another reason why the US army were able to defeat the Indians in warfare was because of their use of Indian scouts.

Use the SuperFact called **Using enemies** to help you finish this part of the answer.

> This helped the army defeat the Indians because ... (iv)

Answering questions: Questions 5 (a) and 6 (a)

What you need to do

In the exam, you must answer **either** both parts of Question 5 **or** both parts of Question 6.

Part (a) of Question 5 and Question 6 will ask you to **explain** something. For example:

> **Describe the importance of the buffalo to the Plains Indians.**

or **Why was the West so lawless in the mid-nineteenth century?**

or **Describe the difficulties of life on the cattle trail in the 1870s.**

How you do it

Let's use the last question for practice. A good answer to this question might start like this.

> One difficulty of life on the cattle trail was rustlers.

> Rustlers wanted to steal the cattle. Sometimes they managed to rustle cattle unseen, sometimes there was fighting. Either way, if they succeeded, the boss lost cattle and so lost money.

The rest of the answer could be organised as below.

Using the SuperFacts on the right, put **one** fact into each box below.

One fact is enough for this exercise, but you should use more than one fact in the exam.

> Another difficulty of life on the cattle trail was homesteaders.

They were a problem because...	(i)

> A third difficulty of life on the cattle trail was managing the cattle.

They were a problem because...	(ii)

An answer like this, listing a number of **difficulties** of life on the cattle trail and giving **details** of how they created difficulties will reach the top level.

Now turn the page to practise.

SuperFacts

Cattle trail problems included attacks by Indians; homesteaders whose land they drove cattle over (fearing damage and cattle ticks); rustlers who wanted to steal the cattle; feeding the cattle (they lost weight, many died).

Results Plus
Top tip

In the exam, students must answer **both** parts of either Question 5 or Question 6. If they answer one part from Question 5 and one part from Question 6, **only one part will be marked**.

Results Plus
Top tip

Make sure that the information you use is **relevant to the focus of the question**. So if the focus of the question is the problems of life on the cattle trail, don't just say *'One problem was the natural dangers.'* Only answers that explain **how this was a problem** will reach the top level.

Now test yourself

Here is another possible question. This is a chance to practise a full examination answer.

Write in each of the boxes to complete the answer.

Use the SuperFacts on the left in your answer.

Describe the importance of the buffalo to the Plains Indians.

SuperFacts

Plains Indians hunted buffalo and used every part of the animal but the heart (this was buried to keep the herd growing). Plains Indians were nomadic, following the buffalo across the Plains. Men hunted the buffalo; women and children cut it up.

Uses for buffalo parts included meat; shoes, clothes, bags, tipis, shields (hide); fuel (dung); food bags (bladder); knives, tools, sledges (bones); blankets, mittens, clothes (fur); hairbrushes (tongue); bowstrings, thread (sinews); soap (fat).

One way in which buffalo were important to the Plain Indians was the way the buffalo migrated.

(iii)

Another way the buffalo were important was that it provided food.

(iv)

A third way the buffalo were important was ... (v)

(vi)

The answer

You can find suggested answers to the tasks numbered (i), (ii), etc., on page 99.

Answering questions: Questions 5 (b) and 6 (b)

Questions 5 (b) and 6 (b) will ask you to set out some **possible** answers to a question, weigh up the factors involved and make (and explain) your own **balanced judgement**.

Examples of questions it might ask are:

> *"The US army was the biggest cause of the destruction of the Indian way of life on the Plains." Do you agree? Explain your answer.*

> *"The cattle industry was one big success story between 1865 and 1895." Do you agree? Explain your answer.*

> You may use the following in your answer and any other information of your own:
> - Most cowboys were unmarried and wanted to drink and womanise when they reached cow towns.
> - 1860: only real law enforcement west of the Mississippi River was 200 vigilante committees.
> - 1892: Johnson County War, cattlemen and homesteaders fought over land.

We will use the question about the success of the cattle industry, and its additional information, to practice our answers.

How you do it

The best answers will look like this.

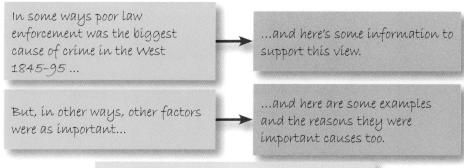

In some ways poor law enforcement was the biggest cause of crime in the West 1845–95 …

…and here's some information to support this view.

But, in other ways, other factors were as important…

…and here are some examples and the reasons they were important causes too.

So, weighing up the various factors that led to crime this is my overall judgement.

Let's try to write this kind of answer. Use the SuperFacts on the right to help you. Start like this:

Poor Law enforcement was one reason for the high levels of crime in the American West 1845–95.

The early towns relied on vigilante committees for law and order. These caught criminals and either lynched them or ran them out of town. Even when sheriffs and marshals were appointed, they were sometimes corrupt. For example, Wyatt Earp was a law enforcer who lost his job several times for breaking the law.

Results Plus
Top tip

Questions 5(b) and 6(b) will not always follow the same pattern. They could ask: if you agree with a statement (for example that one factor was the most important reason for an event); how different things were; why things had a particular effect.

The question types may be different, but they all expect you to:
- use factual information to support and contradict the basic idea in the question
- produce your own judgement on the question.

Top level answers always reach a conclusion about why, how far or how much they agree with a statement.

Signposts
Notice how we use 'signposts' – introductory phrases that mirror the words in the question – to make sure that the answer constantly focuses on the question.

It is vital – especially for this question – that, as you write, you keep using 'signposts' throughout your answer.

SuperFacts

Homesteaders v cattlemen
The railroads brought many homesteaders, given land by the government. At first, some ranchers just drove their cattle across the land, on the old trail. The homesteaders fenced their farms, often with barbed wire. Trails were blocked by homesteads.

Common crimes were cattle rustling; bank robberies (e.g. James Younger gang 1866–82); fence cutting (to get to water or cross fenced land); claim jumping (gold rush); trail robberies (train/stagecoach routes).

Violence in early cow towns, such as Dodge City, was common. Cowboys, after a long time on the trail, gambled, womanised and fought. As towns grew, town councils made rules about carrying guns. From 1870 to 1885, only 39 men died from gunshot wounds. In 1872, Abilene banned cowboys.

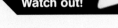
Results**Plus**
Watch out!

Quality of written communication
When your answer to Question 5 (b) is marked, the quality of your written communication will always affect your mark.

To get to the top of each level of the mark scheme you have to:
• write effectively
• organise your thoughts coherently
• spell, punctuate and use grammar well.

Now test yourself
Using the SuperFacts on this page to help you, finish off the answer to the question.

> But poor law enforcement was not the only reason. Another reason why there was so much crime in the West was the conflict over land. One example of this conflict was ... [i]

> This caused crime because ... [ii]

> Another reason ... [iii]

> These were a cause of crime because ... [iv]

But you've not yet finished. This is because the best answers will always:
• take an **overview** of all the arguments
• and come up with their own, **balanced view** on the answer to the question.

In this case, a good answer could finish:

> Overall, I think that poor law enforcement was the most important reason why there was so much crime in the West, because vigilante committees were not always fair or honest and the early sheriffs and marshals were often corrupt. So this caused more unrest and violence. It was only when the federal and state governments created proper law enforcement that crime reduced.

Try writing your own final paragraph using any **other** view of your own.

> Overall, I think that .... was the most important cause of crime in the West because ... [v]

A well-written answer like this, which makes several points for and against, **supported by detail** and finishes with a sensible **balanced conclusion** will reach the top level.

Answers: The American West

Question 1

i) … Indians lived a nomadic lifestyle, moving often from place to place.

ii) … their tipi would be very crowded with the whole family and their possessions in it.

Question 2

i) … he guided migrants, found them shorter routes and helped the army protect them.

ii) … set up trading posts for migrants to get supplies. He guided them and found the Bridger Pass, making their trip shorter. He also set up the Bridger Trail, a safe way to gold in Montana. He guided the army, helping them protect settlers against Indians. So Jim Bridger was a big help to settlers.

iii) Brigham Young was important to the migration of settlers to the West because he successfully led the first Mormon settlers, settled them in Salt Lake City and paved the way for many more Mormon settlers.

iv) He did this by travelling in small groups, on a clear route, giving each person set tasks. At the Salt Lake, he told the Mormons to set up Salt Lake City, using fresh water from streams. Later he helped even more settlers with the Perpetual Emigration Fund. So Young was very important to successful migration.

Questions 3 and 4

i) The Indians traditionally fought with bows and arrows, clubs, spears, and knives. Once they started to fight whites, they began to collect guns, but the army had far more guns. They also had a wider range of guns, including Gatling guns, which were early machine guns. This gave the army an advantage and helped them defeat the Indians.

ii) … their use of forts.

iii) … they were safe bases. In winter, they were warm and safe and allowed the army to attack the Indians, who were disadvantaged when they fought in snow and freezing temperatures.

iv) … they got inside information. For example, they used tribes that were hostile to the Sioux to find out about Sioux tactics, migration and weapons. This helped them defeat the Indians.

Questions 5 (a) and 6 (a)

i) … they were worried about the cattle crossing their land (causing damage and maybe giving the homesteaders' animals cattle tick).

ii) … they didn't want the cattle to lose weight, their meat was their value. But they were taking lots of cattle over the same land, and so the grass got eaten up. Cattle got sick too, and crowded together they spread sickness.

iii) This meant that the Indians had to lead nomadic lives, following the buffalo. Not only does this show just how important the buffalo were, it made an important difference to the way the Indians lived.

iv) They ate every bit of meat on the animal and the intestines and so on. They dried some to preserve it too, to make it last longer.

v) … their use of the hides.

vi) They used the hides to make tipis, shoes and bags. They used them to make clothes and holders for their arrows.

Questions 5 (b) and 6 (b)

i) … between homesteaders and cattle ranchers.

ii) … homesteaders fenced their farms with barbed wire, blocking cattle trails. For example, in 1862, the Johnson County War was a fight between the Wyoming Stock Growers (big ranchers) and homesteaders who had bought ranch land and fenced it off. The Stock Growers lynched some homesteaders. It took the sheriff, 300 men and the US army to restore law and order.

iii) … for the crime in the West was the rapid growth of cow towns.

iv) … cowboys, after a long time on the trail, returned to the cow towns, such as Dodge City, to gamble, womanise, drink and fight.

v) Something like:
Overall, I think that conflict over land was the most important cause of crime. Homesteaders, ranchers, miners, Indians and railway companies were all competing for the same land. This caused fence-cutting, claim-jumping and fights. These were the main crimes.
or
Overall, I think that the cow towns were the most important cause of crime because, at first, they had no law and order at all. After long cattle drives, cowboys drank and fought, to let their hair down. This only stopped when cow towns were properly run after about 1870.

The Unit 2 Exam: A Depth Study

The Depth Study is a chance to study a short period (less than 60 years) in depth. You will have studied ONE of the following:

either   Unit 2A *The transformation of British society c1815–c1851*

or   Unit 2B *The American West c1840–c1895.*

or   Unit 2C *Life in Germany c1919–c1945*

The **structure of the examination** is the same for each. You will always have:

- **one examination paper** lasting **1 hour 15 minutes** in which you will write **five answers**.

The questions will always follow the pattern below.

The number of **marks** you can score for each question is given below.

So is the **time** the examiners recommend you spend on each question (with a few minutes spare for checking your answers).

Q1

4 marks 6 minutes	Question 1 will always give you a source to look at. Then it will ask you to **explain what you can learn about** [something] **from Source A**

Q2

9 marks 12 minutes	Question 2 will ask you to choose one out of two people, groups, events or factors affecting them **Choose one and explain their importance to** [something]

Q3 or 4

12 marks 18 minutes	Both Question 3 and Question 4 will ask you to ... **analyse** something, giving a **description** and **explanation** of it

Q5 (a) or 6 (a)

9 marks 12 minutes	Both Question 5 (a) and Question 6 (a) will ask you to... **Describe** or **explain** [something]

Q5 (b) or 6 (b)

16 marks 25 minutes	Both Question 5 (b) and Question 6 (b) will ask you to make and support a judgement. It might be in the form of a question such as: **Was 'x' the most important cause of** [something]

To help you prepare for the examination, this book does three things.

- First, it helps you with **content**. There is a one-page overview of the content of your Unit. There are also **SuperFacts** for each part of the Unit. (SuperFacts are the key bits of information you need to answer the questions.)
- Secondly, it helps you with **questions**. It explains what you have to do to answer every type of question you will be asked and gives you a chance to test yourself.
- Thirdly, it helps you with **answers**. It provides model answers to all the questions, so you can see how you did.

Overview:
Life in Germany c1919–c1945

Economic reasons:
- recovery under Stresemann too dependent on US loans, hit by the Depression
- rising taxes
- unemployment benefit cut
- rising unemployment

Political reasons:
- the Weimar Republic was unpopular (Treaty of Versailles, economic problems)
- the Weimar Republic's constitution made it weak
- fear of communism
- people wanted a strong, successful government

WHY THE NAZIS CAME TO POWER

Social reasons:
- anti-Jewish and anti-foreign policies popular
- anti-Versailles policies popular
- Hitler's charisma

Tactical reasons:
- propaganda
- violence against enemies
- policies chosen to appeal to many different groups

Children:
- important as the future of the Reich, taught to love Hitler above family
- propaganda in schools
- youth groups

Women:
- to be wives and mothers , not to work (*kinder, küche, kirche*: children, kitchen, church)

LIFE IN NAZI GERMANY

Racial purity/social conformity:
- 'Aryan' race and racial classification with Jews and gypsies as 'sub-human'
- clinics for mentally and physical disabled, where they died from neglect, or were killed
- other, non-racial, 'unacceptable' groups included homosexuals and any religious group that opposed Nazi policies

Controlled by:
- propaganda
- censorship
- secret police
- local Nazi officials

Workers:
- trade unions banned
- Nazi trade union, DAF, controlled working conditions: hours, wages, work
- Nazi control of workers outside work, e.g. Strength Through Joy (leisure activities)

Opponents:
- political opposition banned
- imprisonment (prisons, labour camps, concentration camps)
- execution

Section summary

In 1918, after Germany lost the First World War, the Kaiser abdicated. The new government, the Weimar Republic, signed the hated Treaty of Versailles and had to cope with Germany's economic problems.

Many Germans held the Weimar government responsible for the Treaty of Versailles, the French invasion of the Ruhr (1923) and hyperinflation. There were attempts to overthrow it in 1919, 1920, and 1923. From 1924, the government recovered, mainly due to the work of Gustav Stresemann. First, he stabilised the currency and the economy, then he established better foreign relations. But the Depression of 1929 undid much of Stresemann's work.

The Nazi Party was one of several parties that gained support in the 1920s. By 1923, led by Adolf Hitler, it had its own private army (the SA) and tried to take over the government by force (the Munich Putsch). This failed and Hitler was imprisoned. On his release, the Nazis worked to be elected to power.

SuperFacts 1
The rise of the Nazi Party

SuperFacts are the key bits of information. Learn them and ask someone to test you.

The revolution of November 1918 Sailors at Kiel refused to set out to fight the British navy in late October and marched to Berlin demanding the Kaiser's abdication. They had huge support (due to shortages of raw materials and food, a bad flu epidemic and serious losses in the army). The Kaiser abdicated on 9 November. ●– p.5

The Weimar Republic drew up a new constitution. Everyone over 20 could vote for representatives in the Reichstag and for President. The Reichstag passed laws. The Chancellor ran Germany, but needed Reichstag support. ●– p.6

Proportional representation was the voting method chosen. It gave many political parties seats in the Reichstag. No single party had a majority, so the government was made up of several parties working together (a coalition). ●– p.6

Strengths of the new constitution It was more democratic. Proportional representation meant no single party had all the power. The 18 German states could still pass local laws and run local police forces; central government was not all-powerful. ●– p.6

Weaknesses of the new constitution Free speech laws allowed unchecked criticism of the Weimar constitution. Coalition governments were often weak and collapsed. It was often hard to get the majority vote needed to pass laws, so hard to act quickly and decisively to help the economy. ●– p.6

The Treaty of Versailles The Weimar Republic was unpopular for signing both the armistice that stopped the fighting and the Treaty of Versailles that ended the war. Germany was not invited to the treaty talks, just made to sign what the victorious Allies decided. ●– p.6

The 'War Guilt' clause Article 231 of the Treaty of Versailles made Germany accept that it was responsible for starting the First World War. It was the term many Germans most resented. ●– p.7

Paying reparations put a huge strain on the German economy, already in difficulties because of the cost of the war and inflation. The £6,600 million set by the Allies was so high that the annual payments were impossible to meet. That, and resentment of having to pay, meant Germany fell behind from the start. ●– p.7

Military restrictions No planes, no submarines; no troops in the Rhineland that bordered France (Allied troops based there for 15 years); army limited to 100,000; navy limited to 15,000 and 6 battleships. ●– p.7

Land losses Alsace and Lorraine to France; Upper Silesia, Posen and West Prussia to Poland ('the Polish Corridor', divided East Prussia from the rest of Germany); Northern Schleswig to Denmark and Eupen and Malmédy to Belgium. All overseas colonies lost. Danzig, Memel and the Saar run by the League of Nations. ●– p.7

Germans saw the Treaty of Versailles as unfair. They had not been allowed to take part in the talks before the treaty (which they called a *diktat*, a dictated peace). They said the Weimar government had given the country a 'stab in the back' by signing it. ●– p.8

Reasons for resentment Most Germans did not want to accept war guilt, or pay reparations. They were humiliated by the occupation of the Rhineland and the ban on their troops. Germany lost 10% of its industry (e.g. Saar coalfields) and 15% of its farmland, weakening its economy. ● p.8–9

Widespread resentment Many people at the time felt the treaty was too harsh, even people from the Allied countries that imposed it. US President Wilson tried to base the treaty on his Fourteen Points, which would have been fairer. France and Britain wanted a weak Germany to stop another war. ● p.9

The Spartacists, led by Rosa Luxemburg and Karl Liebknecht, tried to take power in January 1919. The government called on the *Freikorps* to stop the rising. It underlined the weakness of the government, the level of opposition to it, and its need for army support. ● p.10

The government was forced to cut the army, including disbanding the *Freikorps*, by the Treaty of Versailles. In March 1920, the *Freikorps*, led by Wolfgang Kapp, tried to take over the government in the Kapp Putsch. ● p.11

The Kapp Putsch failed because, although Kapp took over Berlin and formed a new government, the people obeyed the Weimar government's order to strike, so Berlin had no gas, electricity, food or coal supplies. Kapp fled to Sweden. It showed that many workers (but not the army) supported Weimar. ● p.11

Adolf Hitler was born in Austria, left school without qualifications and failed to become an artist in Vienna. He was found unfit for the army, but joined when war broke out in 1914 (and they needed more men). He was a good soldier, won medals for bravery and was a good speaker. ● p.12

Hitler was in hospital at the end of the war and always said Germany could have won. He hated the Treaty of Versailles. In September 1919 he went to a meeting of the German Workers' Party, led by Anton Drexler, in Munich. He joined, and was put in charge of propaganda. ● p.13

Hitler took over a local newspaper to publicise his party's ideas. On 24 February 1920, 2,000 people came to a meeting (advertised in the paper) where he announced the new name of the party: the National Socialist German Workers' Party (NSDAP, Nazis for short) and a 25-point programme of aims. ● p.13

Hitler became leader in 1921 and membership grew. In 1922, the Nazi Party had 6,000 members. In 1924 it had 50,000. Much was due to Hitler's use of propaganda; his powerful speeches; and the SA, the party's private army. ● p.14

The SA (*Sturm Abteilung*) were also called 'brownshirts' (their uniform was brown). Led by Ernst Röhm, most were ex-army, many ex-*Freikorps*. They disrupted political opponents' meetings (e.g. communists), often violently. ● p.14

The Nazi programme was designed to appeal to as many people as possible. It was: against the Treaty of Versailles; anti-Semitic (against Jewish people); anti-communist; it promised workers a share in company profits, a share of land and nationalisation of big companies. ● p.14

edexcel ⊞ **key terms**

Freikorps A volunteer group of ex-soldiers used by the Weimar government to crush the Spartacist rising in 1919.

hyperinflation When prices rise very steeply (sometimes several times in one day). In Weimar Germany, it worsened when the government printed too much money to try to solve inflation.

proportional representation A system of elections where seats are divided up among the political parties according to the number of votes each party has.

reparations Compensation payments imposed on most of the losing countries in the First World War by the treaties that ended it. In 1921, Germany's reparations were set at £6,600 million, to be paid in yearly instalments.

soup kitchen A place where soup or other food is given to the needy, either free or very cheaply.

Need more help?
You can find a longer explanation of each SuperFact in your Edexcel textbook, *Life in Germany c1919–c1945*. Look for this symbol ●, which will give you the page number.

ResultsPlus
Top tip

The textbook, and the SuperFacts, give you useful generalisations. But generalising makes all people seem the same, which they are not, and never have been.

When answering exam questions, make sure that you show the examiner that you know that not all Germans thought/wanted the same things or were affected by an event in the same way. So, when discussing the effects of hyperinflation, be sure to consider its effect on different types of people (e.g. pensioners, farmers and businessmen). Even then, be careful about differentiating. So, you can say, 'The value of pensions dropped, so those managing on a pension had less money.' You need to be careful to say 'some businessmen' when discussing its varied effect on businesses.

Hyperinflation To pay off its war debts and reparations, the government printed too much money. When the French occupied the Ruhr, government income fell. The government printed even more money. ● p.19

Hyperinflation hit nearly everyone Pensions and savings became worthless; the food price rise pleased farmers, but rising prices of other goods didn't; wages did not rise with prices, many people could not afford basic foods; the middle class lost faith in the government. ● p.18

Hyperinflation helped some people Some businessmen made money and could pay off loans, even buy up smaller companies; the rich were not helped, but had enough land and possessions to manage. ● p.20

The price of bread In 1919, a loaf of bread cost one mark. In July 1923, a loaf of bread cost 3,465 marks; by November it cost 1.5 million marks. ● p.20

French troops occupied the Ruhr in 1923 because Germany was behind in its reparations payments. The French wanted to take what they were owed in goods and raw materials. The Germans there went on strike or sabotaged factories. This just made the economy, and inflation, worse. ● p.18

The Munich Putsch (1923) was a Nazi attempt to take over government, after Mussolini's success in Italy. People were discontented over hyperinflation and Stresemann calling off passive resistance to the French occupation of the Ruhr. The Nazis had about 50,000 supporters, most of them in Munich. ● p.21

The Munich Putsch failed because the Nazis did not have enough support among the Bavarian government, the people or (crucially) the police. The Nazis and police fought; the police won; Hitler fled, but was later arrested, put on trial and imprisoned in February 1924. The Nazi Party was banned. ● p.22

The Munich Putsch was not a complete failure because Hitler used the trial to publicise Nazi ideas; he only served 9 months of his 5-year sentence; while in prison he wrote *Mein Kampf (My Struggle)*, which set out his aims for the Nazis; he decided on a new strategy – to take power by election. ● p.22

Gustav Stresemann was a key figure in the Weimar Republic's recovery after 1924. He introduced a new temporary currency, the *Rentenmark*. The amount of money printed was limited; hyperinflation stopped. ● p.24, 26

Help from abroad Stresemann ended Germany's isolation from the world (it joined the League of Nations in 1926). He asked for help with the economy and reparations. Negotiations with the USA produced two plans to help economic re-growth: the Dawes Plan (1924) and the Young Plan (1929). ● p.24, 27

The Dawes Plan (1924) re-organised reparation payments and reduced them so Germany had to pay 2,500,000 marks a year. The plan included France withdrawing from the Ruhr and the US making loans (about $3,000 million over the next 6 years, but this made Germany dependent on the US economy). ● p.24, 27

The Young Plan (1929) reduced Germany's reparation payments to 2,000,000 marks a year, extending the time Germany had to pay (58 years). The French agreed to withdraw from the Rhineland 5 years before the Treaty of Versailles said they should. ● p.24, 27

Political recovery by 1929 Support for extremist parties fell (Nazis won 32 seats in the 1924 election, 12 in 1928) **but** opposition was still there and the Dawes and Young Plans created resentment. The government coalition stabilised **but** the problems of proportional representation remained. ● p.28

Economic recovery by 1929 Hyperinflation stopped but the economy relied on huge US loans. Industrial growth set in (at pre-war levels in 1928 for the first time), which boosted employment, **but** many farmers did badly as food prices fell and most industrial growth had slowed by 1929. ● p.28

Nazi election results 1924: 32 seats; 1928: 12 seats; 1930: 109 seats; 1932: 230 seats. In 1932, the Nazis became the largest party in the Reichstag. ● p.30

Nazi Party reforms 1924–28 The Nazi Party ban was lifted in February 1925 and Hitler re-launched it as a national party, with branches (*Gaus*) all over Germany, led by a *Gauleiter*. From 1926 on, there were regular huge rallies, with military-style marches and speeches from Hitler. ● p.32

Nazi organisations The Nazis set up a wide range of organisations aimed at different groups (e.g. the Women's League, the Hitler Youth Movement). The SA tried to change its image, stressing discipline and order, not violence. ● p.32

Nazi propaganda was organised by Josef Goebbels. He used Nazi newspapers, meetings and posters to gain support from groups such as farmers (who were badly hit by the slump in food prices in 1927). Propaganda was also spread at all meetings of Nazi organisations. ● p.32

Support for the Nazis came from the young; skilled workers (e.g. plumbers); workers in towns (but not cities); farmers; middle-class groups (e.g. clerks) who suffered under hyperinflation; middle and upper-class groups who feared growing support for communism; women (heavily targeted by propaganda). By 1928, they had over 100,000 members. ● p.33, 38–9

The US economy collapsed in 1929 The Wall Street Crash is the name given to the huge fall in share prices in October 1929. The US economy had been too dependent on loans; now banks collapsed; many people lost all their savings. The USA could no longer lend Germany money, it needed loans repaid. ● p.34

The Depression was a worldwide economic slump set off by the Wall Street Crash. Many businesses closed, farms cut back on workers. Unemployment rose sharply. By 1932, half of all Germans aged 16–30 were unemployed; unemployment at the end of 1932 was just over 6 million. The Nazis set up soup kitchens. ● p.34

Stresemann died just before the Crash. Lacking a strong leader, the two parties in the coalition government (the Centre Party and the SDP) could not agree on policy. So President Hindenburg was asked to use Article 48 of the constitution (which let him take power in an emergency) to take over. ● p.35

Hindenburg, with Bruning of the Centre Party as chancellor, called the Reichstag less and less often. But they did not solve the crisis. More and more people turned to parties such as the Nazis and the communists. ● p.35

The appeal of the Nazi Party relied heavily on Hitler's speeches and charisma; propaganda (rallies, posters, radio broadcasts, its 8 newspapers); the SA (improved image, but still violent; broke up meetings etc.). ● p.35

Results Plus
Top tip

Read the question carefully and stick to the focus of the question. If you are asked 'Why was the Weimar Republic unpopular **in the years 1919–23**?' you will not get any marks for discussing any problems after that date, however accurately you do so. So, deal with the armistice, the Treaty of Versailles, the economic problems **up to 1923** and the occupation of the Ruhr. You could add that the Republic's unpopularity can be seen by the Spartacists' revolt and the Kapp and Munich putsches.

Need more help?
You can find a longer explanation of each SuperFact in your Edexcel textbook, *Life in Germany c1919–c1945*. Look for this symbol ●, which will give you the page number.

Section summary

Step by step, from 1932–34, Hitler made himself dictator of Germany then set out to create the perfect Nazi state (the Third Reich) using the same combination of terror and propaganda he had used to gain power.

The Gestapo and the SS found, and punished, 'enemies of the state'. The number of arrests, imprisonments and executions (with, or, increasingly, without trial) rose. At the same time, propaganda surrounded the German people daily, aimed at getting them to love and obey Hitler.

Despite the propaganda, there was opposition to Hitler throughout the period. Youth groups (e.g. the Edelweiss Pirates) opposed the Hitler Youth. The churches' reaction was divided, but there was always some church opposition. The army began by supporting the Nazis. By 1944, there was enough army opposition to organise a plot to kill Hitler.

SuperFacts 2
Government of the Third Reich

SuperFacts are the key bits of information. Learn them and ask someone to test you.

Hitler for president? In March 1932, Hitler ran for president. The existing president, Hindenburg, won by 19.4 million votes to Hitler's 13.4 million. It was a setback, but Hitler's votes showed he had wide German support. ● p.46

Step 1: The Reichstag In the Reichstag election of July 1932, the Nazis won 230 seats, becoming the biggest party. The Chancellor, von Papen (Centre Party), held another election, in November, hoping to gain votes. Both his party and the Nazi Party lost seats, but the Nazis still had a majority with 196. ● p.46

Role of Hindenburg Hitler demanded to become chancellor in July 1932, when the Nazis had a Reichstag majority. Hindenburg did not trust Hitler or the Nazis. He spent months keeping Hitler out, during which time the power of the Nazis in the Reichstag and the country became increasingly clear. ● p.46

Stalemate Between May and December 1932 there were three chancellors: Bruning (out May 1932), von Papen (out December 1932) and von Schleicher (resigned January 1933). Neither von Papen nor von Schleicher could get Reichstag support, because of the Nazi majority. ● p.46

Role of von Papen In 1932, Chancellor von Papen only had 68 Reichstag supporters, so was ineffective. He asked Hindenburg to close the Reichstag and rule by decree. Instead, he was replaced by von Schleicher. ● p.46

Hitler and von Papen In November 1932, Hitler made a deal with von Papen to help him become chancellor if he made von Papen vice-chancellor. When von Schleicher resigned, von Papen persuaded Hindenburg there would be civil war if Hitler was not appointed. ● p.46

Step 2: Hitler as chancellor In January 1933, Hindenburg was forced to appoint Hitler as chancellor. The Nazis had much German support. People wanted a stable, effective government to deal with the economic crisis. ● p.46

The Reichstag fire On 27 February 1933, the Reichstag building burned down. The Nazis may have started the fire. A young Dutch communist, Marius van de Lubbe, confessed to the crime. He went on trial with four German communists (arrested later) and was executed. ● p.48–9

Step 3: Emergency decree Hitler persuaded Hindenburg the Reichstag fire was a communist plot. Hindenburg passed an emergency decree that gave the police the power to search houses, arrest people (including the communists in the Reichstag), and hold them without trial for as long as they wanted. ● p.48

March 1933 election In the March 1933 election, the Nazis won 288 seats in the Reichstag. Even without the communists, this was still not the two-thirds of seats Hitler needed in order to change the constitution. ● p.49

The new Reichstag met in March 1933; the SA surrounded the building where it met. They stopped opponents going in; the rest felt threatened. Hitler had made deals with the Centre and National parties to gain their support. ● p.50

Step 4: The Enabling Act (March 1933) The Enabling Act gave Hitler the power to make laws, even if they were against the constitution, without the consent of the Reichstag for 4 years. The promises he had made, and the threat of the SA outside, meant this was passed by 444 votes to 91. ●─ p.50

Step 5: Removal of powerful groups Hitler quickly removed groups that could challenge him in politics or in running Germany: local government, trade unions and political opponents. ●─ p.50

Local government Hitler closed local parliaments (which made their own laws) on 31 March 1933. He re-organised them with Nazis in control, then abolished them in 1934. He didn't want Germans to have local loyalties. ●─ p.50

Trade unions were a threat because they could organise strikes and many did not support the Nazis. On 2 May 1933, Nazis broke into trade union offices all over the country and arrested many officials. The unions were then moved into a single, Nazi-controlled, union: The German Labour Front. ●─ p.50

Political parties On 10 May 1933 the Nazis took over the offices of the Social Democrat Party (its largest rival), destroying its newspapers and taking its funds. The same happened to the Communist Party two weeks later. On 14 July, all political parties except the Nazis were banned. ●─ p.50

The SS (*Schutsstaffel*) were set up as Hitler's personal bodyguard. They grew in size and power with the Nazi Party. They became the Nazi's political police, able to arrest people and imprison them without trial. They ran the concentration camps and later the death camps. ●─ p.51

Step 6: Night of the Long Knives
On 30 July 1934, the SS arrested Röhm and 100 other SA leaders. This purge was because the leader of the SS (Himmler) and Röhm were struggling for power; Röhm (with an SA of about 2 million) was a threat to Hitler; the Nazis needed the SA less than they had done. ●─ p.51

Hitler and Röhm at a rally in 1933, while the SA was still in favour.

edexcel ⠿ key terms

censorship Where the state tells people what they can and cannot say or show in books, newspapers, plays, films etc.

indoctrination Brainwashing people to accept certain ideas.

purge (in the context of this book) To remove opponents from certain groups.

SS A group set up by Hitler in 1925 as his personal bodyguard, the black-uniformed *Schutsstaffel* (SS for short) grew in size and power with the Nazi Party. They were political police, able to arrest people and imprison them without trial. They ran the concentration camps and later the death camps.

Need more help?
You can find a longer explanation of each SuperFact in your Edexcel textbook, *Life in Germany c1919–c1945*. Look for this symbol ●─, which will give you the page number.

Step 7: Death of Hindenburg In August 1934, Hindenburg died. Hitler made himself Führer, sole leader of the Nazi Party and Germany. ●▶ p.52

The cult of Führer Nazi propaganda always showed Hitler as a great leader. Once he was Führer, propaganda increased. All images of him, all of his public appearances, were carefully managed to show him as a hard-working leader, a man of the people who put his country first. ●▶ p.53

Methods of control The Nazis wanted total, willing obedience from people. They knew this would take time; until then they used restrictive laws, terror and indoctrination to control people. Nazi Party wardens (responsible for about 40 households each) gave out propaganda and spied on people. ●▶ p.54

The Nazi police state was based on the Gestapo (the secret police) who spied and used informers against anyone 'suspicious'. They reported political 'crimes' to the SS. 'Enemies of the state' were held without trial, often in concentration camps. In trials, Nazi-picked judges gave Nazi verdicts. ●▶ p.55

Concentration camps Political prisoners were, at first, held in large, disused buildings, but the Nazis soon set up an ever-growing system of SS-run concentration camps. The first was at Dachau, opened in June 1933. They were increasingly used for other 'undesirables', not just political prisoners. ●▶ p.52

'Undesirables' to the Nazis included black people; beggars; gypsies; the disabled; sexual offenders (the Nazis included homosexuals in this group); religious groups and, more undesirable than any other group to the Nazis, Jewish people. ●▶ p.52

Censorship controlled the information people had. Books were burned; radio producers, playwrights, filmmakers and newspapers were told what to say. The Ministry of Propaganda, run by Joseph Goebbels, was in charge. ●▶ p.53

Propaganda was on the radio (about 70% of homes had one by 1939), on posters, in the cinema, at the theatre, in newspapers and at rallies. Hitler felt that repeating messages, over and over, made people believe them. ●▶ p.58

The Berlin Olympics (1936) were the Nazis' chance to show the world how successful and popular they were. They built a huge new stadium (it held 110,000 people). Germany won the most gold medals (33), but Jesse Owens, a black US athlete, won four gold medals. Hitler refused to present them. ●▶ p.59

The Nazis and religion The Nazis were very anti-Jewish, but they were also opposed to all forms of religion, they wanted people to be totally loyal to Hitler and the Third Reich – any religion might bring a conflict of loyalty (e.g. the Catholic Church had a Catholic Youth organisation). ●– p.60

Catholic concordat About two-thirds of Germans were Catholic. In July 1933, Hitler and the Pope signed a concordat (agreement). Hitler agreed to Catholics being able to worship freely if the Pope did not interfere in German politics. But the Nazis took Christian symbols out of schools, then closed Catholic schools. ●– p.60

Catholic protest In 1937, the Nazis made the Catholic Youth illegal. Priests made protests about Nazi actions; hundreds were sent to concentration camps. The Pope felt Hitler had broken the concordat. In 1937, he published a statement 'With Burning Anxiety' criticising the Nazis, but the persecution went on. ●– p.60

Protestants When the Nazis took power, about 2,000 Protestant churches formed a Reich Church (supporting the Nazis). Over 6,000 churches joined the Confessional Church, led by Pastor Niemoller, which spoke out against Nazi policies. Niemoller, and many others, were sent to camps. ●– p.60

The Edelweiss Pirates was a resistance group set up in opposition to the Hitler Youth. They wore checked shirts and dark trousers, read and listened to censored material, wrote anti-Nazi graffiti on walls and, later, helped the resistance movement in the Second World War. ●– p.62–3

The White Rose Group was set up by Professor Huber and two students (Hans and Sophie Scholl) at Munich University in 1941. They leafleted people about German army actions on the Eastern Front in the Second World War (e.g. murder of whole villages), urging them not to support the war. ●– p.62–3

The Scholls were caught by the Gestapo in February and many group members were then caught and brought to trial. All three leaders were executed, along with many others. ●– p.62–3

Army opposition to the Nazis grew after the defeats on the Russian Front. Many soldiers also reacted against the brutality of the SS. ●– p.65

The July Plot On 20 July 1944, von Stauffenberg tried to blow up Hitler at a military conference. The bomb exploded but Hitler was only wounded. Over 5,500 were executed for plotting, including von Stauffenberg. ●– p.65

ResultsPlus
Top tip

When asked to describe the role of a certain group, or the ways a group or different groups acted, **do not** just list what you know about these groups. Produce detail that links them to the focus of the question. So, if asked to describe the different kinds of opposition the Nazis faced in Germany 1933–39, **do not** list opposition outside Germany or outside the time period stated. Discuss different opposition groups (e.g. the Eidelweiss Pirates, the White Rose Group and church organisations) and how and why they opposed the Nazis.

Need more help?
You can find a longer explanation of each SuperFact in your Edexcel textbook, *Life in Germany c1919–c1945*. Look for this symbol ●–, which will give you the page number.

Section summary

The Nazis had clear ideas about the state they wanted to build. Women would be wives and mothers. Men would be workers and soldiers. Children, the long-term future of the state, were to be brought up to obey the state willingly and to be completely loyal to it, valuing it even above their parents.

The Nazis wanted to reduce unemployment rapidly, and did so by creating work through their rearmament programme and by building a growing number of 'invisible unemployed' through their policies towards women, Jews and other groups.

Nazi racial policies, especially their division of society into Aryans and 'undesirables', meant that there were many groups in Germany that the Nazis did not welcome and actively persecuted. Once Germany was at war their level of persecution increased, especially that of Jewish people, who they attempted to wipe out in their 'final solution'.

SuperFacts 3
The social impact of the Nazi state

SuperFacts are the key bits of information. Learn them and ask someone to test you.

Women in the Weimar Republic had been given the vote; by 1933, almost 10% of Reichstag deputies were women. Many women worked, including in professions such as law and medicine. Some had equal pay to men. ●▬ p.71

Nazi views on women Nazis thought women should focus on the traditional *kinder, küche, kirche* (children, kitchen, church). They frowned on women working, or wearing make-up or trousers, as many women did in 1933. ●▬ p.71

Women and work The Nazis pushed women out of professions such as law and teaching. This made jobs for men and reduced unemployment. The Nazis had to call women back to work in 1936, and during the war, when there was a labour shortage. They kept women's wages at two-thirds of men's. ●▬ p.72

Women and marriage The Law for the Encouragement of Marriage (1933) lent couples who married 1,000 marks (a month's wage) if the wife left work. For each child, they were let off a quarter of the loan. This boosted marriage, large families and women staying at home. ●▬ p.72

Women as mothers The German Women's Enterprise (a Nazi organisation) gave classes and radio broadcasts on good motherhood. The Nazis gave medals to women with children on Hitler's mother's birthday. The medals were bronze for 4–5 children, silver for 6–7, gold for 8 or more. ●▬ p.72

Obeying the Nazis The German Women's Enterprise had 6,000 members, and marriage and the birth rate rose under the Nazis, while the number of working women fell until the Nazis needed them for war work. But only a small proportion of women had more than three children. ●▬ p.73

The 'ideal' Nazi family, painted by a Nazi-approved artist in 1939.

Nazi education was planned to make Germany strong. Hitler wanted children to grow fit and healthy; girls to be good wives and mothers; boys to be soldiers. He said the purpose of education was 'to create Nazis'. Lessons began and ended with the 'Heil Hitler' salute. ●– p.74

Nazi schools All children went to school until they were 14. All schools had the same curriculum: PE took up 15% of school time. Lessons taught Nazi views (e.g. race studies taught Aryan superiority). Boys learned science and maths, while girls learned to sew and cook. ●– p.74

Propaganda in schools From 1935, all textbooks had to be Nazi-approved and new ones were full of Nazi propaganda. Teachers had to join the Nazi Party. History books glorified the Nazi rise to power and blamed economic problems on the Jews. Books for race studies also taught anti-Semitism. ●– p.74

Nazi youth movements *Deutsches Jungvolk* (Young German Folk, 10–14) and *Jungvolk* (Hitler Youth, 14–18) were training boys for the army. The *Jung Mädel* (Young Girls, 10–14) and *Bund Deutscher Mädel* (League of German Maidens) were for girls and taught homemaking. Everyone kept fit. ●– p.77

Hitler Youth Laws (1936, 1939) made it difficult not to join, then compulsory to join, a Hitler Youth group. Membership rose from 5.4 million in 1936 to 8 million in 1939. During the war, they worked to raise money for the war and for charities (e.g. Winter Relief) and helped in the emergency services. ●– p.78

The New Plan (1933), run by Hjalmar Schacht, aimed to make Germany self-sufficient. He limited German imports and made trade agreements for countries to supply raw materials to Germany and buy German goods. By 1935, Germany's production was up 50% on 1933. ●– p.81

The 4-Year Plan (1936) Hitler wanted Germany ready for war in 4 years, so the economy focused on rearmament and the raw materials of war: rubber, oil, steel, cloth and fuel. Factories tried, not very successfully, to make them synthetically (e.g. petrol and rubber from coal, cloth from pulped wood). ●– p.82

Expanding industry From 1936, Herman Göring came to control German economic policy. New industrial works were built all over the country for rearmament, mining and metalworking. All these new industries needed workers; many came as forced labour from concentration camps. ●– p.82

Unemployment figures for January were 6 million in 1933; 3.8 million in 1934; 2.9 million in 1935; 2.5 million in 1936; 1.8 million in 1937; 1.1 million in 1938 and just over 300,000 in 1939. ●– p.80

---

edexcel ⠿ key terms

invisible unemployment When some groups are not included in unemployment statistics. Under the Nazis, the invisible unemployed included women, Jews, prisoners in camps (many of whom were actually used as unpaid forced labour), people on 6 months' compulsory service in the RAD.

Need more help?
You can find a longer explanation of each SuperFact in your Edexcel textbook, *Life in Germany c1919–c1945*. Look for this symbol ●–, which will give you the page number.

edexcel key terms

Aryanisation Taking away businesses, then homes, from Jewish people and giving them to 'suitable' Germans who had been classed as 'Aryan'.

subhuman The name given by the Nazis to all races but the Aryan race. They divided subhumans into various levels of acceptability, with those 'unworthy of life' (which included Jewish people and gypsies) at the bottom.

undesirables The name given by the Nazis to people who they felt were not welcome in the Third Reich for reasons of race, health or behaviour.

Top tip

The different Nazi organisations for workers can be confusing, because their initials are the initial letters of the German words for that organisation. Try to think of ways that help you remember them. For example, say to yourself:

'The DAF replaced trade unions, was that a DAFt idea?'

Employment came from state public works (e.g. autobahns); taking jobs from women and Jews (not included in unemployment statistics); sending opponents to camps; expanding industry for self-sufficiency and rearmament; building a huge army (100,000 in 1933; 1,400,000 in 1939). ● p.80, 83

The National Labour Service (RAD) was begun by the Weimar Republic. From 1935, all men aged 18–25 had to do 6 months' low-paid work in the RAD. They did public works (e.g. draining marshes for farmland, building public buildings). By 1939, they had built 7,000 miles of autobahn. ● p.80

The German Labour Front (DAF) was the state-run Nazi replacement for trade unions. It set working hours and wages and encouraged workers to work together for Germany, rather than thinking of their own situation. Under the DAF, working hours went up by an average of 6 hours a week. ● p.85

Standard of living Wages rose 20%; but the price of food rose too (most people were eating less in 1937 than in 1927). More people were working; but they worked longer and had few rights. ● p.80

Farmers Some farmers had help from RDF schemes and all benefited from the Nazis keeping production low so prices rose. However, some farmers lost workers to the factories and the army. ● p.86

Businesses Small businesses had supported the Nazis. Some benefited from the Nazis closure of Jewish businesses. Big businesses benefitted most. There were no trade union problems and rearmament led to extra production. However, the state controlled wages, profits, and what was produced. ● p.86

Nazi views on race The Nazis had a racial hierarchy. 'Pure' Aryans (Hitler's invented race) were blond-haired, blue-eyed Europeans. Then came races such as eastern European Slavs. Below them came black people, gypsies and Jews. ● p.88

The master race The Nazis wanted to build a 'master race' in Germany, weeding out all groups but Aryans and weeding out the unhealthy Aryans too. They also controlled Aryan breeding. The SS, chosen for Aryan characteristics, were only allowed to marry women with similar characteristics. ● p.88

Burdens on the community The Nazis wanted everyone to contribute to society. People who were mentally or physically disabled were taken from their families and put into 'care homes'. This institution first ill-treated, then killed, their 'patients'. Vagrants were put to forced labour. ● p.90

Early persecution of Jews In 1933, the Nazis organised boycotts of Jewish businesses and began to 'Aryanise' them. Jews could not work in government. They were banned from restaurants and public places (e.g. parks, swimming pools). ●▶ p.91

The Nuremberg Laws (1935) said Jews were not German citizens, so could not vote or have passports. They could not marry Aryans. Later, Jews could not join the army. From 1936, they had to carry identity cards and have 'Jewish' names. Jewish professionals (e.g. doctors) could not have Aryan clients. ●▶ p.91

Kristallnacht (the Night of Broken Glass) Over the night of 9 November 1938, the Nazis took revenge for a young Jew shooting a Nazi official in Paris. The Gestapo, SA, SS and Hitler Youth all took part in raids on Jewish homes, synagogues and businesses. ●▶ p.93

Effects of Kristallnacht Nazi statistics say 815 shops, 191 synagogues and 171 homes were damaged; 76 synagogues demolished; 91 Jews killed; 20,000 Jews sent to concentration camps. The Jewish community was fined 1 billion marks; Jews were banned from owning or running businesses. ●▶ p.93

The Second World War meant the Nazis could be more extreme in their treatment of Jews (world opinion mattered less). As Germany captured Poland and other countries, it faced a bigger Jewish population (there were 3 million Jews in German-occupied Poland). ●▶ p.94

Ghettos In 1939, all Jews had to move into ghettos: walled-off areas of cities, kept apart from other people. The Nazis kept ghettos overcrowded and poorly supplied with water, food and electricity. Warsaw ghetto (October 1940–April 1942) had a population of 140,000–340,000. About 5,000 died every month. ●▶ p.94

Einstatzgruppen Germany invaded Russia in June 1941. Special murder squads (*Einstatzgruppen*) followed the army as it advanced, rounding up and killing whole villages of Jews, who were forced to dig a mass grave before being shot. By 1943, they had murdered about 2 million people. ●▶ p.94

The Wannsee Conference (January 1942) laid out the 'final solution' to the 'Jewish problem'. Death camps were to be set up, all in Poland, none in Germany. Jews were to be taken there from ghettos, concentration camps and labour camps and murdered. The first of these was Belzec (March 1942). ●▶ p.95

Death camps There were four death camps (Belzec, Sobibor, Treblinka and Chelmno) and two death camps with a nearby labour camp (Auschwitz-Birkenau and Majdanek). ●▶ p.95

Camp deaths By the time the camps were liberated in 1945 about 6 million Jews, 500,000 gypsies and countless other prisoners had been starved to death, worked to death, gassed or shot by the Nazis. ●▶ p.95

ResultsPlus
Watch out!

Be clear about the different sorts of camps set up by the Nazis.

concentration camps All the camps that were run by the SS with prisoners who were arrested and kept without trial.

labour camps These provided forced workers. Some held foreigners and, once war broke out, prisoners of war. Others held a mixture of prisoners, divided into different groups. Some were small, some enormous; the map on page 95 of your textbook only shows the biggest. However, they all provided workers.

death camps Set up in 1942, these camps existed simply to kill people, most of them Jews or gypsies. Prisoners were given forced work, but only until it was their turn to die.

Need more help?
You can find a longer explanation of each SuperFact in your Edexcel textbook, *Life in Germany c1919–c1945*. Look for this symbol ●▶, which will give you the page number.

An **inference** is a judgement made from the source, which is not directly stated by it.

A **supported** inference is one that uses detail from the source to prove the inference.

Consider this example:

Source A: 'Sue pushed her friend, Liz, off the swing. Liz's mother was angry and said she was going to tell Sue's mother what had happened.'

Question: What does Source A tell us about Sue?

Information: *Source A tells us Sue pushed Liz off the swing.* [This is directly stated in the source, so it's not an inference.]

An inference could be: *Source A tells me that Sue is in serious trouble and is likely to be punished.* [The source does not directly tell us this, but we can infer that it is likely.]

A supported inference could be: *Source A tells me Sue is in serious trouble and likely to be punished. I can infer this because she pushed Liz off the swing and Liz's mum was cross and was going to tell Sue's mum, who would be cross too.* [An inference, with supporting details quoted from the source.]

When you are asked what you can learn from a source, make sure you do not just describe the source. To get the best marks you have to make an inference from the source, work out something extra from it. You must also tell the examiner what part of the source led you to make the inference.

Answering questions: Question 1

What you need to do

Question 1 will always ask:

> **What can you learn from Source A about... [something]?**

The best answers:
- make **inferences** from the source [*see Top tip box*]
- and **support** those inferences with detail from the source.

Here are a **source** and a **question** for you to study.

Source A: A photograph of the Nazi SS during the Nuremburg Rally of August 1933.

What can you learn from Source A about the Nazi Party in 1933?

How you do it

(i) Write the inference you can make from the supporting detail provided.

(ii) Write the supporting detail which goes with the inference provided.

Inference	Supporting detail
One thing I can infer from Source A is that ... [i]	I can infer this because the source shows lots of SS men, they are well equipped and have perfect, expensive-looking uniforms and lots of banners.
I can also infer from Source A that the Nazi Party thought that appearing to be strong would help its political success.	I can infer this because ... [ii]

An answer like this, with **two** inferences, both **supported by detail** in the source will reach the top level.

Answering questions: Question 2

Question 2 will always show you two people, two groups of people, or factors or two events.

It will then say:

> *Choose one and explain the importance of this person/group/factor/event for... [something]*

What you need to do

The best answers will not just write all they know about the person, group, factor or event, but will instead:

- say what the importance of the person (or group, factor or event) was

- give supporting detail about their actions to explain how the person (or group, factor or event) was important.

How you do it

Take this question as an example:

> *The boxes below show two people. Choose one and explain the importance of that person to German politics 1919–45.*

> Gustav Stresemann   Paul von Hindenburg

Let's choose to write our answer about **Gustav Stresemann**.

We will use the SuperFacts on the right in our answer. Remember the focus of the question, the **importance** of Stresemann. Remember to provide **supporting detail** for what you say.

Importance	Supporting Detail
Gustav Stresemann was important to German politics 1919–45 because he stabilised the currency, ended Germany's isolation and got international help with reparations.	For example, Stresemann stabilized the currency by abolishing the worthless German currency and introduced the Rentenmark. He ended isolation by getting Germany accepted as a member of the League of Nations in 1926. He got help with reparations by negotiating the Dawes Plan and the Young Plan; these reduced the reparations burden. All this was important because politics became more peaceful 1924–29 and support for the extreme parties fell.

An answer like this, which states the **importance** of the person and gives **detail** to **explain** it, will reach the top level.

The best answers may be longer than this one, but they must follow this pattern.

Now turn the page to practise this yourself.

SuperFacts

Gustav Stresemann was a key figure in the Weimar Republic's recovery after 1924. He introduced a new temporary currency, the *Rentenmark*. The amount of money printed was limited; hyperinflation stopped.

Help from abroad Stresemann ended Germany's isolation from the world (it joined the League of Nations in 1926). He asked for help with the economy and reparations. Negotiations with the USA produced two plans to help economic re-growth: the Dawes Plan (1924) and the Young Plan (1929).

The Dawes Plan (1924) re-organised reparation payments and reduced them so Germany had to pay 2,500,000 marks a year. The plan included France withdrawing from the Ruhr and the US making loans (about $3,000 million over the next 6 years, **but** this made Germany dependent on the US economy).

The Young Plan (1929) reduced Germany's reparation payments to 2,000,000 marks a year, extending the time Germany had to pay (58 years). The French agreed to withdraw from the Rhineland 5 years before the Treaty of Versailles said they should.

Political recovery by 1929 Support for extremist parties fell (Nazis won 32 seats in the 1924 election, 12 in 1928) **but** opposition was still there and the Dawes and Young Plans created resentment. The government coalition stabilised but the problems of proportional representation remained.

The answer
You can find suggested answers to the tasks numbered (i), (ii), etc., on page 123.

SuperFacts

Hitler became leader in 1921 and membership grew. In 1922, the Nazi Party had 6,000 members. In 1924 it had 50,000. Much was due to Hitler's use of propaganda; his powerful speeches; and the SA, the party's private army.

The SA (*Sturm Abteilung*) were also called 'brownshirts' (their uniform was brown). Led by Ernst Röhm, most were ex-army, many ex-*Freikorps*. They disrupted political opponents' meetings (e.g. communists), often violently.

Methods of control The Nazis wanted total, willing, obedience from people. They knew this would take time; until then they used restrictive laws, terror and indoctrination to control people. Nazi Party wardens (responsible for about 40 households each) gave out propaganda and spied on people.

The SS (*Schutsstaffel*) were set up as Hitler's personal bodyguard. They grew in size and power with the Nazi Party. They became the Nazi's political police, able to arrest people and imprison them without trial. They ran the concentration camps and later the death camps.

The answer
You can find suggested answers to the tasks numbered (i), (ii), etc., on page 123.

Now test yourself

Here is another possible Question 2.

We will use the SuperFacts on the left in our answer.

The boxes below show two groups. Choose one and explain the importance of that group's work for the success of the Nazi Party.

> The SA 1923–34

> The SS 1934–45

First, write an answer about **the SA** in the box below.

Importance	Supporting detail
The SA were important to the Nazi Party (1923–34) because … (i)	The way the SA did this was … (ii)

In the exam you must just choose **one** topic.

But, just for practice, write about the **SS** in the boxes below.

This time, we haven't started you off with 'signpost' phrases. We've left you to write your own 'signposts' to show the examiner exactly how you are answering the question.

Importance	Supporting detail
(iii)	(iv)

Answering questions: Questions 3 and 4

In the exam, you have to answer **either** Question 3 **or** Question 4.

Questions 3 and 4 will always ask you to **analyse** something, describing and explaining it. For example: the questions may ask you why something happened.

The questions will then always give you some information to help you with your answer.

For example, Question 3 or 4 could say:

> **Why was there so much unrest during the early years of the Weimar Republic?**

You may use the following in your answer and any other information of your own.
- In August 1919, the Weimar Republic adopted a new constitution.
- In June 1919, the Treaty of Versailles was signed.
- By 1923, Germany could no longer pay its reparations payments.

What you need to do

The best answers will:
- **state reasons** why there so much unrest.
- after each reason, **give details to explain** how each reason caused unrest.

You do not have to use the information given in the box under the question.

However, that is a good place to start.

How you do it

Take the question above as an example.

Use the SuperFacts on this page and the next to help you.

We have used important, introductory words at the start of our answer. These words are 'signposts' which help the examiner see how you are answering the question.

You could start by using the first piece of information given in the question, like this.

One reason why there was so much unrest during the early years of the Weimar Republic was the Weimar constitution.

The Weimar constitution caused unrest in several ways. First, free speech allowed criticism of the Weimar government. Second, because of the constitution, the early governments of the Weimar Republic were coalitions. They were often weak and collapsed. It was hard for them to get the majority vote needed to pass laws. Third, there were groups like the Spartacists who opposed the Weimar constitution. In 1919, they tried to overthrow the Weimar Republic.

ResultsPlus
Top tip

Questions 3 and 4 will always be followed by some useful information to help you with your answer. This extra information could be useful information, a quote or a picture.

It will be useful and relevant information. You can use other information as long as it is **relevant to the focus of the question**. You do not need to do so.

Answers that are closely tied to the focus of the question, rather than talking around it, will reach the top level.

SuperFacts

Weaknesses of the new constitution
Free speech laws allowed unchecked criticism of the Weimar constitution. Coalition governments were often weak and collapsed. It was often hard to get the majority vote needed to pass laws, so hard to act quickly and decisively to help the economy.

The Spartacists, led by Rosa Luxemburg and Karl Liebknecht, tried to take power in January 1919. The government called on the *Freikorps* to stop the rising. It underlined the weakness of the government, the level of opposition to it, and its need for army support.

SuperFacts

Germans saw the Treaty of Versailles as unfair. They had not been allowed to take part in the talks before the treaty (which they called a *diktat*, a dictated peace). They said the Weimar government had given the country a 'stab in the back' by signing it.

Reasons for resentment Most Germans did not want to accept war guilt, or pay reparations. They were humiliated by the occupation of the Rhineland and the ban on their troops. Germany lost 10% of its industry (e.g. Saar coalfields) and 15% of its farmland, weakening its economy.

Hyperinflation hit everyone Pensions and savings became worthless; the food price rise pleased farmers, but rising prices of other goods didn't; wages did not rise with prices, many people could not afford basic foods; the middle class lost faith in the government.

Hyperinflation helped some people Some businessmen made money and could pay off loans, even buy up smaller companies; the rich were not helped, but had enough land and possessions to manage.

The price of bread In 1919, a loaf of bread cost one mark. In July 1923, a loaf of bread cost 3,465 marks; by November it cost 1.5 million marks.

French troops occupied the Ruhr in 1923 because Germany was behind in its reparations payments. The French wanted to take what they were owed in goods and raw materials. The Germans there went on strike or sabotaged factories. This just made the economy, and inflation, worse.

The answer
You can find suggested answers to the tasks numbered (i), (ii), etc., on page 123.

Now test yourself

We have used the first piece of extra information in the question to start the answer.

Now you use the second and third pieces of information in the question to finish it.

> Another reason why there was so much unrest during the early years of the Weimar Republic was the Versailles Treaty.

> The Versailles Treaty caused unrest because … (i)

> A third reason why there was so much unrest during the early years of the Weimar Republic was… (ii)

> This caused unrest in several ways… (iii)

Remember, you can add your **own reasons** to those given in the question.

- For example, in answer to this question, you could say:

> Another reason there was unrest during the early years of the Weimar Republic was the French occupation of the Ruhr.

Use the SuperFact called **'French troops occupied the Rhur'** to help you finish this part of the answer.

> This caused unrest because … (iv)

Answering questions: Questions 5 (a) and 6 (a)

In the exam, you must answer **either** both parts of Question 5 **or** both parts of Question 6.

Part (a) of Question 5 and Question 6 will ask you to **explain** something. For example:

> *What were the key features of Nazi education policy?*

or > *Describe the ways the Nazi Party was able to win support in the years 1929–32.*

or > *Describe how Nazi economic policies changed Germany 1933–39.*

Take the **third** question above as an example. The best answers to this question will:

- state the **difficulties** of life on the cattle trail
- use **detailed information** to **explain** each difficulty.

How you do it

Let's use the last question for practice. A good answer to this question might start like this.

> One change was that industrial output grew.

> Nazi economic policies made this change in various ways. The 'New Plan' (1933) aimed to make Germany self-sufficient. Trade agreements helped imports of raw materials and sales of manufactured goods. German production rose by 50% from 1933 to 1935. The '4-Year Plan' boosted output of war materials like rubber, oil, steel, cloth and fuel. Later, Göring used labour from the camps to boost output.

The rest of the answer could be organised as below.

Using the SuperFacts on the right, put **one** fact into each box below.

One fact is enough for this exercise, but you should use more than one fact in the exam.

> Another change introduced by Nazi economic policies was to reduce unemployment.

> They did this by... (i)

> Another change introduced by Nazi economic policies was to control the labour force with the DAF.

> This was a change because... (ii)

An answer like this, listing a number of ways in which Nazi economic policies changed Germany and giving details of how they did so will reach the top level.

Now turn the page to practise.

SuperFacts

Unemployment figures for January were 6 million in 1933; 3.8 million in 1934; 2.9 million in 1935; 2.5 million in 1936; 1.8 million in 1937; 1.1 million in 1938 and just over 300,000 in 1939.

Employment came from state public works (e.g. autobahns); taking jobs from women and Jews (not included in unemployment statistics); sending opponents to camps; expanding industry for self-sufficiency and rearmament; building a huge army (100,000 in 1933; 1,400,000 in 1939).

The German Labour Front (DAF) was the state-run Nazi replacement for trade unions. It set working hours and wages and encouraged workers to work together for Germany, rather than thinking of their own situation. Under the DAF, working hours went up by an average of 6 hours a week.

ResultsPlus
Top tip

In the exam, students must answer **both** parts of either Question 5 or Question 6. If they answer one part from Question 5 and one part from Question 6, **only one part will be marked**.

ResultsPlus
Top tip

Make sure that the information you use is **relevant to the focus of the question**. So if the focus of the question is to describe how the Nazis won support in the years 1929–32, only answers that explain **how** what they did won them support will reach the top level.

Now test yourself

Here is another possible question. This is a chance to practise a full examination answer.

Write in each of the boxes to complete the answer.

Use the SuperFacts on the right in your answer.

Describe the key features of the Nazi policy towards women in Germany 1933–45.

One feature of Nazi policy towards women was about marriage.

(iii)

Another feature of Nazi policy towards women was about motherhood.

(iv)

Another feature of Nazi policy towards women was about ... (v)

(vi)

SuperFacts

Nazi views on women Nazis thought women should focus on the traditional *kinder, küche, kirche* (children, kitchen, church). They frowned on women working, or wearing make-up or trousers, as many women did in 1933.

Women and work The Nazis pushed women out of professions such as law and teaching. This made jobs for men and reduced unemployment. The Nazis had to call women back to work in 1936, and during the war, when there was a labour shortage. They kept women's wages at two-thirds of men's.

Women and marriage The Law for the Encouragement of Marriage (1933) lent couples who married 1,000 marks (a month's wage) if the wife left work. For each child, they were let off a quarter of the loan. This boosted marriage, large families and women staying at home.

Women as mothers The German Women's Enterprise (a Nazi organisation) gave classes and radio broadcasts on good motherhood. The Nazis gave medals to women with children on Hitler's mother's birthday. The medals were bronze for 4–5 children, silver for 6–7, gold for 8 or more.

The answer

You can find suggested answers to the tasks numbered (i), (ii), etc., on page 123.

Answering questions: Questions 5 (b) and 6 (b)

In the exam, you have to answer **either** Question 5 **or** Question 6. So if you answered Question 5 (a) you **must** answer Question 5 (b).

Questions 5 (b) and 6 (b) will ask you to set out some **possible** answers to a question, weigh up the factors involved and make (and explain) your own **balanced judgement**.

Examples of questions it might ask are:

> *How important was the Second World War as a cause of the 'Final Solution'?*
>
> *"Economic depression was the main reason Hitler came to power." Do you agree? Explain your answer.*

You may use the following in your answer and any other information of your own:
- In February 1933, the Reichstag building burned down.
- In March 1933, the Reichstag passed the Enabling Act.
- In August 1934, President Hindenburg died.

This is the question we shall use to practise our answers to Questions 5 (b) and 6 (b).

How you do it
The best answers will look like this.

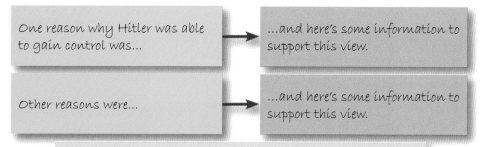

| One reason why Hitler was able to gain control was... | → | ...and here's some information to support this view. |

| Other reasons were... | → | ...and here's some information to support this view. |

So, my view is that there was no one reason, many different factors worked together to help Hitler come to power.

In the margins of this page, there are SuperFacts to help us. So let's start like this.

> One reason why Hitler was able to gain complete power over Germany 1933–34 was that he exploited the Reichstag Fire in February 1933.

> This helped Hitler increase his power over Germany because he persuaded Hindenburg the fire was a communist plot (a Dutch communist, van de Lubbe, was arrested for it). Hindenburg passed an emergency decree that gave the police the power to arrest people and hold them without trial for as long as they wanted. This meant Hitler could arrest and lock up his communist opponents in the Reichstag, which obviously increased his hold on power.

SuperFacts

The Reichstag fire On 27 February 1933, the Reichstag building burned down. The Nazis may have started the fire. A young Dutch communist, Marius van de Lubbe, confessed to the crime. He went on trial with four German communists (arrested later) and was executed.

Step 3: Emergency decree
Hitler persuaded Hindenburg the Reichstag fire was a communist plot. Hindenburg passed an emergency decree that gave the police the power to search houses, arrest people (including the communists in the Reichstag), and hold them without trial for as long as they wanted.

ResultsPlus
Top tip

Questions 5 (b) and 6 (b) will not always follow the same pattern. They could ask: if you agree with a statement (for example that one factor was the most important reason for an event); how different things were; why things had a particular effect.

The question types may be different, but they all expect you to:
- use factual information to support and contradict the basic idea in the question
- produce your own judgement on the question.

Top level answers always reach a conclusion about why, how far or how much they agree with a statement.

ResultsPlus
Top tip

Signposts
Notice how we use 'signposts' – introductory phrases that mirror the words in the question – to make sure that the answer constantly focuses on the question.

It is vital – especially for this question – that, as you write, you keep using 'signposts' throughout your answer.

SuperFacts

The new Reichstag met in March 1933; the SA surrounded the building where it met. They stopped opponents going in; the rest felt threatened. Hitler had made deals with the Centre and National parties to gain their support.

Step 4: The Enabling Act (March 1933) The Enabling Act gave Hitler the power to make laws, even if they were against the constitution, without the consent of the Reichstag for 4 years. The promises he had made and the threat of the SA outside meant this was passed by 444 votes to 91.

Step 7: Death of Hindenburg In August 1934, Hindenburg died. Hitler made himself Führer, sole leader.

ResultsPlus
Watch out!

Quality of written communication
When your answer to Question 5 (b) is marked, the quality of your written communication will always affect your mark.

To get to the top of each level of the mark scheme you have to:
- write effectively
- organise your thoughts coherently
- spell, punctuate and use grammar well.

The answer
You can find suggested answers to the tasks numbered (i), (ii), etc., on page 123.

Now test yourself
Using the SuperFacts on this page to help you, finish off the answer to the question.

> Another reason why Hitler was able to gain complete control over Germany 1933-34 was the Enabling Act passed when Hitler was able to keep opponents from voting because ... (i)

> The Act was important for his control over Germany because... (ii)

> Another reason was the death of President Hindenburg.

> Hindenburg's death helped Hitler increase his power over Germany because... (iii)

But you've not yet finished. This is because the best answers will always:
- take an **overview** of all the arguments
- and come up with their own, **balanced view** on the answer to the question.

In this case, a good answer could finish:

> Overall, I think the most important reason why Hitler was able to gain complete power over Germany 1933-34 was the Reichstag Fire. This made people frightened of a communist plot and gave Hitler the excuse to increase his own power. It set the scene for all the other ways through which he increased his power.

Try writing your own final paragraph using any **other** view of your own.

> Overall, I think the most important reason why Hitler was able to gain complete power over Germany 1933-34 was... (iv)

A well-written answer like this, which makes several points for and against, **supported by detail** and finishes with a sensible **balanced conclusion** will reach the top level.

Answers: Germany c1919–c1945

Question 1

i) ... the Nazi Party was well funded in 1933.

ii) ... they are parading SS men who look more like an army than politicians. They have uniforms and helmets, just like soldiers, to make them look strong.

Question 2

i) ... they helped the party to grow.

ii) ... they were Hitler's private army; they used violence to disrupt opponents' meetings, e.g. communist meetings.

iii) The SS were important to the Nazi Party 1934–45 because the Nazis wanted total, willing obedience from people. The SS helped them achieve this.

iv) The way the SS did this was by acting as the Nazi special police. They could arrest people and imprison them without trial. They ran concentration camps and, later, the death camps.

Questions 3 and 4

i) ... the German people thought it was unfair. They did not want to accept war guilt, have a smaller army or pay reparations. They also lost 10% of their industry and 15% of their farmland. All this fuelled unrest. Germans called the treaty a 'diktat' – a dictated peace. They said the Weimar government had given the country a 'stab in the back' by signing it.

ii) ... hyperinflation.

iii) most Germans were hit hard by hyperinflation. Pensions and savings became worthless. Rising prices meant many people could not afford basic food. The price of a loaf of bread rose to 1.5 million marks in 1923.

iv) ... the Germans there went on strike or sabotaged factories. This just made the economy, and inflation, worse and this caused more unrest.

Questions 5 (a) and 6 (a)

i) ... not counting all the people in prison camps as unemployed and also re-arming (so more industrial jobs) and building up their army (more soldiers needed).

or

... by public works and also by, for example, taking jobs from women and Jews and re-arming.

ii) ... they banned trade unions and controlled all wages and working conditions from the centre.

or

... they took control of working hours; these went up by an average of 6 hours per week in the 1930s.

iii) They believed the tradition role of women: children, kitchen and church. In 1933, the Law for the Encouragement of Marriage lent couples who got married 1,000 marks (about a month's wage) and for each child they had they were let off a quarter of the lean. So after four children and there was nothing to pay back.

iv) They wanted women to be good mothers. The German Women's Enterprise gave classes and radio broadcasts on good motherhood. The Nazis gave medals to women with children on Hitler's mother's birthday. Women got gold medals for 8 children or more.

v) ... women at work.

vi) The Nazis pushed women out of professions such as law and teaching. This made jobs for men and reduced unemployment. But their policy changed in 1936. They needed women back at work. This was even more important in the war years. But they didn't pay women as much as men for the same job.

Questions 5 (b) and 6 (b)

i) ... he'd arrested the communists and the SA stopped opponents going in to vote; the ones they let go in felt threatened. The Enabling Act was passed by 444 votes to 91.

ii) ... it gave Hitler the power to make laws, even if they were against the constitution. He didn't need the consent of the Reichstag for 4 years, so this made him much more powerful.

iii) ... Hitler was able to make himself Führer, sole leader of the Nazi Party and Germany.

iv) Something like:

...the Enabling Act. The Reichstag Fire and the death of Hindenburg gave Hitler the opportunity to increase his power, but the Enabling Act legally gave him complete control of Germany.

or

... the death of Hindenburg. The fire and the Enabling Act gave Hitler powers, but it was when he became the Führer that Germany was, for the first time, led by one man, Hitler.

Published by Pearson Education Limited, a company incorporated in England and Wales, having its registered office at Edinburgh Gate, Harlow, Essex, CM20 2JE. Registered company number: 872828

www.pearsonschoolsandfecolleges.co.uk

Edexcel is a registered trademark of Edexcel Limited

Text © Pearson Education Limited 2010

The rights of Jane Shuter, John Child, and Paul Shuter have been asserted by them in accordance with the Copyright, Designs and Patents Act of 1988.

First published 2010

10 9 8 7 6 5 4 3

British Library Cataloguing in Publication Data

A catalogue record for this book is available from the British Library.

ISBN 978 1 84690 590 2

Produced by Paul & Jane Shuter Ltd for Edexcel

Edited by Lauren Bourque

Typeset by AMR Design Ltd (www.amrdesign.com)

Illustrated by AMR Design Ltd

Picture research by Thelma Gilbert

Printed in Malaysia (CTP-VP)

Acknowledgements

We would like to thank Cathy Warren for her invaluable help in the development of this book.

The publisher would like to thank the following for their kind permission to reproduce their photographs:

Alamy Images: Oasis/Photos 12 107, The Art Archive 82, World History Archive 48, North Wind Picture Archives 86, David Levenson 19, Pictorial Press Ltd 13, 24, 49; Bridgeman Art Library Ltd: French Photographer 58, 71; iStockphoto: 25; TopFoto: The Granger Collection 27, 56, 69, 110, Topham / Fotomas 28, Topham Picturepoint 90, 114, Topham Picturepoint 90, 114

Cover images: Front: Corbis: Bettmann

All other images © Pearson Education

Details of written sources:
p28, Schools Council History 13-16 Project, *Medicine Through Time: Book Two: The beginning of change*, Holmes McDougall, 1976; p52, Peter Stanley, *For Fear of Pain: British Surgery, 1790–1850*, Clio Medica/ Wellcome Institute, 2003; p71, W. J. Bishop, *A Short History of Medicine*, Oldbourne Book Co. Ltd, 1962; p73, Charles Singer and E. Ashworth Underwood, *A Short History of Medicine*, Oxford University Press, 1962; Jerry D. Gow, 'A Time to Heal', *Transactions of the American Philosophical Society*, Vol 89, Part 1, 1999; Royal Australian College of Surgeons,www.surgeons.org/Content/NavigationMenu/CollegeResources/ HeritageandArchives/CollegeCollections/TreasureoftheMonth/Treasure_of_Mon16.htm; Roy Porter, *The Cambridge Illustrated History of Medicine*, Cambridge University Press, 1996.

Every effort has been made to contact copyright holders of material reproduced in this book. Any omissions will be rectified in subsequent printings if notice is given to the publishers.